PRINCIPLES OF THE PRECEPTS

FURTHER ZEN RAMBLINGS FROM THE INTERNET

SCOTT SHAW

BUDDHA ROSE PUBLICATIONS

Principles of the Precepts
Copyright © 2020 by Scott Shaw
www.scottshaw.com
ALL RIGHTS RESERVED

Cover Photograph by Scott Shaw
Copyright © 2020—All Rights Reserved

Rear Cover Photograph of Scott Shaw
by Hae Won Shin
Copyright © 2020—All Rights Reserved

First Edition 2020

This book contains material protected under International and Federal Copyright Laws and Treaties. Any unauthorized reprint or use of this material is prohibited. No part of this book may be reproduced or transmitted in any form or by any means, electronic or mechanical, including photocopying, recording, or by any information storage and retrieval system without express written permission from the author or publisher.

ISBN 10: 1-949251-35-7
ISBN 13: 978-1-949251-35-7

Library of Congress: 7982473112

10 9 8 7 6 5 4 3 2 1
Printed in the United States of America

PRINCIPLES OF THE PRECEPTS

Introduction

Here it is, *The Scott Shaw Zen Blog 18.0,* originally presented on the *World Wide Web.* All of the writings presented in this book were written between September and December of 2020.

As was the case with the previously published volumes based upon *The Scott Shaw Zen Blog;* entitled: *Scribbles on the Restroom Wall, The Chronicles: Zen Ramblings from the Internet, Words in the Wind, Zen Mind Life Thoughts, The Zen of Life, Lies and Aberrant Reality, Apostrophe Zen, The Abstract Arsenal of Zen and the Psychology of Being, Zen and Again: The Metaphysical Philosophy of Psychology, Tempest in a Teapot and the Den of Zen, Buddha in the Looking Glass, Wo Ton' of the Blue Vision, Zen and the Psychology of the Spiritual Something, Pyrophoric Zen, Fragments of Paradox, Zen: Traversing the Entity of Non-Entity, Zen and the Ambient Echo: The Psychological Philosophy of Being, Paritical Zen and the Life Science of Becoming No Thing,* and *Obscurist Occulto: Hiding from the Definition of Meaning* this volume is presented exactly as it was viewed on *scottshaw.com* with no rewriting, punctuation, or typo corrections. From this, we hope you will receive the original reading experience.

This volume of internet ramblings is presented with the date and time listed as to when each blog was originally posted. Also, the blogs in this volume are presented from last to first. With this, we hope to present a transcendence back through time as opposed to an evolving evolution. In addition, we left out the traditional *Table of*

Contents in an attempt to leave this volume with a much more free-flowing reading experience.

Okay, there's the information and the definitions. Read on… We hope you enjoy it. And, be sure to stayed tuned for the ongoing *Scott Shaw Zen Blog @ scottshaw.com.*

That's Just Who They Are
10/Dec/2020 10:38 AM

People are who they are. A lot of people claim that they can change but is that a reality? More common is the person who feels that there is no need to change. Perhaps a person who holds this mindset is the truest being as they are true to themselves. For better or for worse that is who they are.

Most people find themselves in a state of evolutionary flux. As they become the person they are to become they are influenced by a billion (or more) influencers. But, no matter what the influence is, at their root there is the person that they are—the personality that they possess. No matter the influences, no matter what someone else gets someone to do, at the core of each person is the who they truly are.

Think about the people you have met in life. Some people you are immediately attracted to. This is unusually based on their physical, outward appearance. You like the way the look. You like the style of clothing they wear. There are millions of physical attractions as one passes through life. For example, think about how many people you find attractive as you pass through a shopping mall. Once the physicality either leads to a meeting or a meeting occurs for an entirely different reason, then who that person truly is comes into play.

Think about a time you met someone that you now have known over a long period of time. Think back to that first meeting. Think about the first conversation you had with that person. What was your impression of that individual? Think about it. Chart it out.

Now, progress a year, two years, ten years, or a lifetime later, what do you think about that person now? Have you maintained the same impression of that person that you had when you first met them? The answer for most is probably, no. You got to know them better and you began to see their attributes and their faults. How did that advanced understanding come to define your relationship with that person? Did it bring you closer or did it ultimately make you walk away?

It is no secret that most people present an idealized image of themselves to the external world and to new people that they meet. Some people flat out lie about who they are and pretend to be something that they are not. How about you? How do you present yourself to the world?

The thing is, the longer you know a person, the more their true nature is revealed. The more you associate with someone, as time and situations occur in your relationship, the person they truly are is revealed. This may come in moments of frustration, conflict, lust, or just them perhaps revealing that they are a very selfish, self-centered, jealous, violent, irrational, or bitchy individual. When you witnessed this for the first time, was that their first time they behaved like that? Of course not. That is just who they truly are. That is who they have always been. It is simply the first time that you were allowed to witness it.

Not everyone operates from a life-position of negative emotions. Many are truly pure, kind, and caring individuals. The people who hold and possess these personalities are the easiest to chart from the outset of any relationship because they are not operating from a position of pretext. They simply are who they are with little or nothing to hide or conceal. Sadly, people like this are few and far between, however. More commonly, we encounter people who mask their true desires and their true personality.

So, what does this leave us with? What does this leave you with?

Think about the people you know—think about the people you have known for a long time; are they perfect? Are they the perfect incarnation of a human being as defined in your mind? Probably not. They have their personality faults just as we all do. More than likely, you have witnessed, you have encountered, you have defined their flaws and you have chosen to accept them for who they are though who they are may not be the ideal person you think they should be.

How about you? How much time do you spend defining your personality flaws? How many of your flaws illustrate who and what you truly are and how you behave towards others? Do you ever attempt to try to correct your personality flaws or do you let them dominate any life-relationship you enter into? How many flaws do your friends and your family have to forgive for them to remain in a relationship with you? And, do you ever contemplate or question any of this?

All life is based in who a person is. All relationships are based in accepting who a specific person is. People can become better. The only problem is, most people do not try to become better. They do not choose to attempt to raise themselves and their human interaction skills to the level where they can be a conduit for all things good in life.

Do people meet you, like you, and truly know who and what you actually are? Do you hide your true inner darkness? Or, are you a vehicle of light and goodness?

All life begins with you and who you are. All life-interactions begins with what you are willing to accept in the behavior of others. If we all take the time to truly reflect on what we are, how we got to be here, and how we act and react towards others, not only do we become a better more evolved person but everyone who meets us can find solaces in what we project to the world.

This is your life. Who are you? What are you? Why do you do what you do and why do you behave towards others in the manner that you behave? If you don't know, then you don't know. If your negative emotions control you and cause you to act in unacceptable ways, then they control you. That means you are out of control.

Life is your vehicle. This is all you have. Your interactions with others will come to define your life. How you behave, how you accept the behavior of others comes to be the final piece in the puzzle of your life. So, what are you going to do? What are you going to allow others to do? You need to know or you will never know.

What is the Cost of Time?
09/Dec/2020 11:29 AM

Okay… So, I write this blog. It has evolved over time. …The way I write and when I write, it has changed as time(s) have changed. Once upon a time, I used to toss out all kinds of personal stuff about where I would be, when I would be there, and the like. I thought that was what you were supposed to do. Then, the weird stuff started with some weird people. Most were cool. They would seek me out as they just wanted to meet me, talk about whatever, be in one of my Zen films, or something like that. AOK. But, there were also a few weird stalkers out there—in real life and on the internet. I detailed this in the intros to the first couple of published books taken from the writing presented in this blog. A couple of times, that nonsense caused me to rethink blogging altogether, and for a while I would quit.

Also, my blog writing used to be different… I would write for a while and then I would stop for six months, a year or so, and then come back to it. Now, I write a lot more. Well, I always write. Back then, a lot of my writing went to magazines (remember those?) or for chapters in books and stuff. But, times change and reality changes…

I suppose I could leave all of my blog-orientated writings up here on this site forever and ever but that just seems like it would be way too much information. So, whenever there gets to be a certain amount of new STUFF it gets pulled down and published in book form.

From what I gather, some people read this blog frequently, while others just happen onto it and read it once or from time to time. All good! For those who you have been reading this blog for a long time you may remember back several years ago when I would occasionally blog about this very loud, very rude neighbor I had. He would be loudly preaching to his followers via Skype, telling them all this New Age bullshit, stolen straight out of someone else's books, and when he was not doing that he was screaming, *"Fuck me, fuck me, fuck me, fuck me and mine"* over and over and over again while stomping his feet on the floor like a four year old. He really ruined my life for like two and a half years and the life of all of the neighbors. The reason I mention him is that he used to always read this blog. Scary... But, I'll get more into him and his antics in a second.

BTW: Why do some people get to ruin the lives of other people and never have to pay them back? I should write a blog about that. ☺

Like I always say, just because you do the time or pay the karmic price for the crime you committed that does not mean that you undo that crime to the person you unleashed that crime against, nor does it mean you ever compensate that person for how you damaged their life... Not right, buts that's reality.

Anyway... Before I get too far off point... It is not uncommon that someone who reads this blog remembers some blog I wrote way back when and if it never made it to the Greatest Hits segments of this blog it comes down. Sometimes people contact me asking about some specific blog they remember way back in the way back when and they want me to send a copy of it their direction. Again, I write a lot of stuff, sometimes I remember the piece, sometimes I don't. Sometimes I can track it down, sometimes, if the description is far too vague, I can't. But, the main component in all of that/this is time. It takes time. Time, which I am happy to provide if it will help someone, but time that is gone, nonetheless. What is the cost of time?

What I am saying here is that the writings are all out there. They are all in book form. The books are easily found on this site and easily purchased from Amazon or your local bookstore. The time and the place and the creation dates of the blogs easily located.

The reason I mentioned that really bad neighbor is that, I used to hear him telling people to buy my blog books, read them, and then return them like he did. I heard him because he was so loud... This always made me shake my head... What a dick! What a thief! As I consider that stealing... ...Buying something with the mindset that you are going to use it and then intentionally return it... The point being, the stuff is published. It's easy to find and not very expensive. So, if there is some blog that I wrote that inspired you, you learned something from, it illustrates how you think I'm a jerk, you want to look back and see what I was writing about Back Then, or whatever, it is in print. You can get it. And, thank you if you pick up a copy of one or all of my Blog Books!

You know, giving is always giving. That is one of the greatest things about life, you can always find a way to give and help a person if you care enough to try.

Giving is always giving, just like taking is always taking. Gifts are given. There are those people who are true givers. They try to help all those they can. Then, there are the takers like the aforementioned bad neighbor. Which one are you? Who do you want to be? Think about it... Think about the time you ask of someone. Think about the time you take from someone. Think about the time it takes for someone to give you something. What is that time worth to you? And, what are you willing to pay for it? Think about the time you give and the time you take. What is the cost of time?

* * *
07/Dec/2020 10:23 AM

Think about some something that you really cared about once upon a time. Some something that is now gone from your life.

Maybe it was stolen, maybe it broken, maybe you had to sell it because you needed money, maybe you gave it away to someone you cared about but they did not appreciate it.

Truly bring that object clearly into your mind's eye.

What if you still had it?

What if it never left your life?

What would your life be like?

How would your life have evolved differently?

Now question, can you get it back?

Can you somehow replace it?

If you can, what would that mean to your life?

How would it make your life better or different?

If you can get it back, why don't you try?

Life is defined by what you define as precious.

Though all objects are only as temporal as the person who cares about them. But, if you care about something and it makes your life better, that something can change everything in your life. If you can own it, you should.

* * *
07/Dec/2020 10:11 AM

You can only witness the world through your own perspective but it is you who decides how vast your perspective actually is.

*   *   *

07/Dec/2020 10:05 AM

When was the last time you said something positive about someone you do not like?

Try it and your entire life experience may change.

* * *

07/Dec/2020 10:01 AM

If you have to proclaim that you are, *"A Something,"* in life you will forever be nothing as something can always be taken away from you.

Nothing is freedom.

*   *   *

07/Dec/2020 09:49 AM

Your windows are your key to the world. How often do you clean your windows?

Locked into a Pattern
07/Dec/2020 08:06 AM

For each of us, we define our life by what we do. For each of us, we define our life by how we do things. *"That's me." "That's who I am." "That's what I think." "That's what I do."*

The problem with this style of life behavior is, however, new experiences are limited and held back from occurring by the accepted and the expected. You do what you do the way you do it but it never changes. You think what you think the way you think it but it never changes.

Sometimes new experience grabs a hold of us. We are forced into it. For some, they love this occurrence. For others, most in fact, they hate it. They fight and they complain and they resist. Why? Because they are so locked into the previously experienced, they do not want to encounter the new.

How about you? Where are you in your life? How much NEW is in your life? How much NEW do you let it? Do constantly seek out the NEW? Or, do you run away from it believing that what you do and the way you do it is the best of the best and that is who you are for better or for worse?

Take a moment right now and think about your life. How much NEW do you let in? How much NEW, in comparison to how much already done and expected, have you encountered in the past week, month, or year?

If you actually take the time to study this Life Factor, (something that very few people do), you will come to have a deep insight into who and what you are and why you find yourself where you find yourself in your life.

The person who seeks out the NEW is not better than the person who hopes to continually experience the same thing over and over and over again but they do live a life providing a much broader base of experiences leading to a more complete understanding of their life, the life of others, directing them towards a deeper overall understanding of humanity.

This is your life. This is your choice to make. You can choose to do the same thing the same way over and over and over again or you can allow yourself to encounter the NEW. This choice can be made at any point, at any moment in your life. Your life. Your choice. New or old, what are you going to decided to do right now?

* * *
07/Dec/2020 07:18 AM

If you don't know the reason why then you don't understand anything.

Free Form Philosophy
06/Dec/2020 07:49 AM

I am frequently asked the question, *"Where do I get the ideas for the blogs and the aphorisms that I write?"* I don't really have an answer. They just come to me. Rarely, are they ever planned for. Yes, sometimes they are written long before they are published but there is never an outline or anything like that created before they go pen to paper.

This kind of stuff is just who I am. I've been doing it forever. It is just the kind of things that I think about. From my earliest memories forward, I have always studied the human condition. I have forever peered into the motivations for why people do what they do and why I do what I do. For whatever karmic logic, that is just who I am.

I have also been asked, *"Why did I not pursue a career in psychology or something like that?"* The truth be told, I don't really like people. Though I hope to help the all and the everyone to the best degree of my ability, whenever I can, I find most people to be so self-involved, so uncaring, so self-serving, so selfish, so lost in their own melodrama, (though most will deny this fact), that it is hard for me to focus on caring about them one-on-one. What's left? This. These blogs and my other writings. …A way for me to help those who wish to take the time to read these words; possibly providing someone with some food for thought that may cause them to take a new look at their life, what they do, why they do it, why other people do what they do, and this life experience on the whole.

So, for those of you have wondered, there is your answer. A bit of insight into Scott Shaw. ☺

* * *
06/Dec/2020 07:24 AM

If you have to make up excuses and tell lies about the things that you have previously done then you shouldn't have done them in the first place.

Think before you do.

Movies and the Things You Never Know
05/Dec/2020 08:48 AM

  For anyone who has ever created a movie, or any creative project for that matter, there are things that take place that only the people who were there truly understand. For everyone else, it is simply speculation, projection, or guessing, at best. This is why I forever find it troubling when someone describes what took place on the set of one of my films when they were not on the set. They don't know! Yet, there they are, telling the world what they believed happened. But, it did not.

  People believe. That is one of the realities of life. They hear and they think it to be true. But, look around at life. Look at all the things you have listened to. Think of all the things you have heard. How many of those things were the truth spoken by someone who lived it verses how many of those words were simply someone's interpretation of what they believed might have happened? Me, personally, whenever I hear someone talking about something they have no true experiential knowledge about, I tune out. Why listen to them? They know nothing!

  I think to some of the movies I have created or been a part of. There is the completed product. There is what the audience sees. There is what the critics interpret and judge. But, so many times I am confronted with the fact that what people construe, what people think they know about what took place behind the scenes is so far off the mark that it is almost impossible to calculate.

  I can think of one film that I have rarely spoken or written about to use as an example…

In the world of independent filmmaking, there has long been this seeming need to bring people onto a project that have some name recognition. This is most commonly done in order to hopefully boost potential sales. I have never been a fan of this process. For me, as a filmmaker, I have always been much more happy to introduce the unknown actor to the world. Yes, in some cases, I have become friends with, *"Name talent,"* so that is a completely other ballgame. But, *"The Name,"* for name sake, in independent filmmaking, has always proved problematic.

I remember my Zen Filmmaking brother, Donald G. Jackson, was at the helm of this one film we created. The shooting title for the film was, *"It's Showtime,"* but Don never liked that title. The script was written by Mark Williams (RIP).

Don was always a bit *Star Struck.* Me, growing up in Hollywood and all that... ...Seen it all before... Anyway, Don decided to cast Don Stroud. Great guy! Great choice! Plus, the actor who become famous from the movie, *Grease* and the TV show, *Taxi,* Jeff Conway for the, *"Name talent,"* of the film. Now, by this point in time, Jeff had a sorted past and was known to be a problem on the set. Yet, Don wanted him even though I questioned his judgment. On the set, it's time for Jeff to come on and do his part. He refused to leave his trailer even though he was a paid a lot of money to be there. Everyone was trying to coax him out, to little avail. The guy was obviously high as that is what he did. Don even ended up being a totally dick and yelling at the great actor Don Stroud due to his frustration. If I was Don (Stroud) I would have told him, *"Fuck you,"* and walked off the set. But, he was a total professional. Conway, on the other hand...

Anyway, Don finally talked Conway out of his trailer. He delivered a piss-poor performance, constantly forgetting his lines, but that is what you get when you hire a person of his mentality. He wanted to be treated like a star. He wanted to be pampered and babied. He was in the film, he was a, *"Name talent,"* but at what cost?

Now, this is a very obscure film. I could go into what happened with the master copies of it and all that but, again, that is just something that if you weren't there you would never truly understand. In the past, I have been pointed to people who actually viewed the film and have spoken about this film. All I can take is a moment or two of that kind of stuff because immediately I realize they are totally wrong in what they say. They weren't there! They don't know! Yet, they talk...

So, what is all this discourse about? It is about the fact that what YOU live is what YOU live. If you have not lived it, why are you even thinking about it? It was not your life. What you think you know about it is only speculation at best. Why waste your Life Time contemplating anything that you were not a true part of?

Life is about experiencing. Life is about living your life. If you are attempting to live your life via the doings of someone else, all you have done is to turn your life over to them. You are attempting to live your life through them. What is accomplished by interpreting the experiences of someone else? ...Experience you have not and cannot ever truly understanding.

Live your own life. Experience what you experience. Don't attempt to chart the anything of anyone else because you were not there. Don't waste your time attempting to understand it, because you can't. All you can do is live your own moment as fully as possible. This is the place/the space; the state of mind where living a GOOD life is formed. Forming the Pure Mind is not out there. …Thinking you know and telling the world about something that you never personally experienced. It is found by living a good life as inquisitively and as positively as possible.

Live your own life. Talk about what you know. Speak about what you have personally experienced. Then your truly knowledge, your inner-realization may be rightly exhibited to the world.

* * *

04/Dec/2020 01:17 PM

Your life is measured by how much time you have wasted.

* * *
04/Dec/2020 09:23 AM

When you look out across the horizon are you studying what is out in the distance or are you locked into your own mind thinking about experiences that have already transpired?

Everybody Wants to Be a Badass but Nobody Wants to Say They're Sorry
03/Dec/2020 11:45 AM

  I always find driving to be one of the most revealing exercises for peering into the human psyche. I'm not talking about the crazy driving that goes on in places like Bangkok or Delhi, just the everyday driving that goes on in places like here is L.A. It seems that when people drive they instantly reveal their true human nature. Yes, some are very passive but most, it seems, are just the opposite. They revel their true nature of selfishness, thoughtlessness, ego, and anger.

  Today, I was driving down a street and the car in front of me decided to come to a complete stop. Obviously, they didn't look in their mirror to see if someone was behind them, they just decided to come to a complete stop. I, of course, honked. They drove on, obviously going intentionally very slow. When I finally passed them, the guy in the driver seat glared at me. This made me smile. You did something inconsiderate and wrong yet you want to focus your anger onto me.

  As I always say, you should really think about who you're dealing with before you decide to break hard with someone. Now, I'm not just talking about me but there are a lot of highly trained fighters out there who would be more than happy to take someone apart. I even have a couple of friends who, though they were never formally trained in the fighting arts, are serious scrappers. I've witnessed them tear some people up. In one case it was a so-called fifth degree black belt in Taekwondo. Yet, when someone is in a car they somehow become some all powerful force to be reckoned with. I've witnessed both men and women behaving in the manner. But why? Why can't someone just admit that they did something wrong that affected the life of someone else in some negative manner? Why can't they just say, *"Sorry?"*

Again, this goes back to the fact of driving being a very revealing source to peer into a person's character. There are many people out there who simply do not give a fuck about anyone else. There are many people out there that believe the world should revolve around them. There are many people out there that are so based in a state of anger, due to dissatisfaction with their own life and their own life circumstance, that they seek any means to lash out. Plus, there are those people out there who believe they are a superior fighter so they want to take their abilities to the street via any means possible. But, I've seen more than a few of people who possess this mindset get their asses handed to them in a street fight.

So, what can we learn from all of this? …Learn aside from the obvious that driving is one of the most revealing forms of interpersonal psychological analysis. From a personal perspective, we can learn who we are. Ask yourself, how do you react behind the wheel? How do you react to others behind the wheel? How do you treat others and how do you think about other drivers? How do you react when you do something wrong and someone honks at you?

In terms of understanding human psychology, we can learn by observation. We can learn the limitation of most human beings. We can witness, through their behavior, the way people view their life, the life of others, and how they allow something so momentary as a horn being blown to take control over their entire frame of mind which may or may not lead them down the road to unfolding negative life events.

In life, everything is your choice: how you react to life, how you react to the actions of others, how you think about and how you treat others.

The question you must constantly ask yourself is, how are you treating others, how are you thinking about others, how are you allowing others to control your life?

The truth be told, you can behave anyway you choose to behave. This is your life. What you do and what you encounter is highly defined by how you react to life and to other people in your life. So, how do you behave in life? Are you in control of your emotions and your actions? Or, are you out of control of your emotions. Do you allow your emotions and the actions of others to dominate how you encounter life?

Your life. Your choice.

Next time you take a drive, take the time to analyze who you truly are. Next time you take a drive, watch the actions and the reactions of others. From this, you can truly learn a lot, not only about yourself but also about the all and the everything of humanity.

* * *
01/Dec/2020 03:28 PM

How much is your happiness worth?

What is the cost to you?

What is the cost to everyone else?

No Horse in the Race
AKA Nothing to Lose
01/Dec/2020 09:41 AM

Have you ever been in one of those situations when you are working for someone else or doing something for someone else but it is their gig, it is their business, it is their project? Sure, they invited you, they asked you to help them out, they hired you to do the job, but it is not your business, it is not your project, you will not win or lose based upon the outcome. In this place/in this space, yes, you may do the best job that you can but do you really care? If that person fails that does not mean that you fail. You can move on. You can take on the next job offer, the next friend's request. It is they who stand to win or lose, not you. Thus, this provides you a level of freedom that the person you are doing the task for does not possess. They must accomplish that end-goal. But, for you, there is no long-term, life-changing pressure.

The problem when you hire someone is that this is his or her mindset. Yes, they may do the job they were hired to do so they will be paid, but, at the end of the day, they are not the person in the bull's-eye. Yes, the person you ask to help you do something may do it to the best of their ability because they care about you, but they are not the one who's life will change if it is not completed with a level of excellence.

Think about your own life, think about the people who have hired you or asked you to do something for them. What was your mindset? How did you behave? Define the feelings that you felt. Think about how you felt about your superior. Define how you felt about the job at hand. Truly bring into focus the thoughts that you had. For most, the experience of this experience is very much the same. There is the feeling of, *"It's someone's else's situation."* Maybe you care about the job that you do because that is just the kind of person that you are but you know that the doing of this deed is not the definition of your life.

Now, switch this around. Think about a time that you asked someone to do something for you. If you were, at some point in your life, in a position of power, think about a time when you hired someone. Compare the feelings of that experience to the one where you were not the center-point. How did you feel about expecting someone to do something for you? How did you feel about the necessity of having that person getting the job done right? Did they? Did they do a good job? Did they do a bad job? How did that make you feel? If they did do a bad job, if they did mess up and/or ruin your project, how did that make you feel? And, did you/could you recover from it? In some cases, the doings of someone else keeps a person from ever recovering.

In life, there is always one person in the position of frontal power. There is the one person who envisioned the project and that one person who is in control of the project. Few projects can be accomplished alone, however. Thus, other people must be brought in to assure success. Some people come into the project caring—they hope to get it done right. Others bring in their own agenda and/or their own attitude of disinterest. Some even attempt to make a project fail. In all of these cases there are two points of view: the yin and the yang if you will. There is the person who is at the pinnacle, the person who must get the project completely correctly, because their life and their life evolution depends on it. Then, there is the everyone else; the person/the people who may come onboard the project, for whatever reason, but they do not/cannot care that much about it because it does not ultimately define their life.

To look at this situation from a broader perspective, one can say that you hope to find people who care—you hope to hire people who care. But, even if a person does care, they will forever hold a certain level of disinterest and lack of responsibility because, whatever that project or that job is, it is not their envisionment. It is not their conception. It is not their life definition.

As a person, you can choose to enter into any project with the promise of providing excellent service. But, no matter how much you try to do, in the back of everyone's mind they know whatever project that is not their own they are not ultimately responsible for. Blame can be placed, people can be fired, friendships may be destroyed but no matter how you slice it, someone else's project is never your own. You've got to know this, you've got to understand this, you've got accept this at the outset of ever either launching a project or working on one. There are two points of view. There are two mindsets. And, no matter how much you wish the two minds to merge as one this will never ultimately occur.

System of Belief
30/Nov/2020 09:43 AM

Everybody believes in something. Even the people who do not believe in a greater power have a belief. The belief of nothing. Some people keep their beliefs to themselves. Others project their beliefs out to anyone who will listen. No matter the case, one thing is true; belief is only belief, it is not necessarily fact.

Here lies the problem; most people cannot differentiate the difference between belief and fact. Thus, they present their beliefs as fact and as most people do not possess the level of discrimination to differentiate between the two, life becomes a convoluted mess of varying beliefs affecting the lives of the all and the everyone.

Think about the people who believe in Christianity; they hold their set of core beliefs based upon what is written in the Bible. Think about the people who are followers of Islam; they hold their set of core beliefs based upon what is written in the Koran. These are two religions that both claim to hold the truth. Millions upon millions of people believe in both of these religions. Are they same? No. They each possess varying teachings and they each teach that one should rebuke the nonbeliever. So, which religion is right?

You see, here lies the essence of belief; it is based upon an accepted concept in the mind of the believer. Is it right or is it wrong? Who can say because it is solely based upon what one believes? Who can be the actual judge?

In life, some people loudly proclaim what they believe. From a psychological perspective, the reason the people who proclaim their beliefs the most loudly is based upon the fact that they hope to be viewed as a, *"Knower."* But, what do they actually know? All they know is what they believe but if what they believe is based upon nothing more than what they think they know then by that very definition their belief is flawed as it is nothing more than an opinion and an opinion is nothing more than a personal belief based upon self-defined assumptions.

To take this to a more personal perspective, every now and then I will see someone on Facebook or some other social platform posting how he or she is going to clean house of the people that are negative or spouting something they do not like or believe in. Frequently, you hear about people facing online bullying, being trolled, or being attacked by some entity out there in cyber space based upon someone not liking a person, what that person creates, what they say, or what they stand for. During the recent election season, here in the U.S., which was very divisive, I have seen so many people posting very negative, very biased, opinions based solely upon belief—based solely upon what they heard from someone else that propped up what they already believed. In fact, some people I observed were actually banned from Facebook, Twitter, and other social platforms for posting things that apparently were not permitted. But, the problem is, <u>everything</u> is based upon belief. The only problem arises when someone decided to broadcast that belief and someone else does not like it. But, if most things are based upon what an individual personally believes, and not based upon fact, who should hold the power to judge what is right and what is wrong?

From a person perspective, as a creative person, (for lack of a better term), my work and myself have been the subject of some people's beliefs. Not always, but sometimes, what people have said or written about my work or myself was complete wrong. It was totally false. Yet, due to their belief, which was not based upon fact, only opinion, they put what they thought out there to the world. From this, others have believed what they concocted. Not fact. Just belief. Yet, it is present for the world to see. This behavior is the sourcepoint for one of the modern world's great problems.

I imagine we have all experienced situations such as this to varying degrees. For some of you out there, reading this, I imagine that you are one of the vocal ones, presenting your belief(s) to others or to the entire world as a whole. For those of you who do this, either on a small or a large scale, do you ever contemplate the fact that what you are thinking, equaling what you are saying, is nothing more that a belief that originated in your own mind? And, if you do understand this fact, do you predicate what you are proclaiming with a statement to that affect? Do you tell people what you are saying is just an opinion? Or, do you state what you state as if it were based in fact when all that is being said is simply an assessment concocted in your own mind?

Most people never take a look at their beliefs. Most people never study what was the impetus or the causation factor for their beliefs. They just believe that they know what they know. But, if you don't know why you know what you know, if you don't know why you present your sometimes false-opinion(s) as fact then you are not only doing a disservice to yourself but you are doing a disservice to the entire world because you are desecrating truth and replacing it with nothing more than your personalized system of belief.

* * *
29/Nov/2020 02:04 PM

If you have to say you're sorry that means you weren't thinking about the other person in the first place.

*　　*　　*

27/Nov/2020 09:57 AM

You can always tell the people who are insecure, unfulfilled, and unaccomplished. They say negative things about other people.

You can always tell the people who are secure, fulfilled, and accomplished. They say positive things about other people.

* * *
25/Nov/2020 09:42 AM

Most people develop and then follow the same patterns of behavior throughout their life.

It is for this reason that very few people are willing to evolve.

How about you?

* * *

25/Nov/2020 09:41 AM

You can suggest to a person what they should change about themselves but if they do not want to listen then all will stay the same.

* * *
25/Nov/2020 09:40 AM

Does your positivity proceed you?

Does your negativity proceed you?

*   *   *

24/Nov/2020 03:56 PM

Have you ever noticed how those people who embrace a negative lifestyle or want to live in denial about what they have or have not done always denounce a person who lives a positive lifestyle?

Who Have You Saved?
24/Nov/2020 09:02 AM

We live in a world of desire. We live in a world of beliefs. We live in a world of opinion. We live in a world of conquest. We live in a world of people doing things that hurt the life of other people. But, who have you saved?

Most everyone can chart what they want from life and what they want from some specific person. Most everyone can chart what they think about a certain subject and what they think about a particular person. Most everyone can chart how they feel about the world, a government, a politician, a sport's player, a musician, an actor, or the person next door. But, how does any of this help anyone?

Most everyone can tell you what they hope to achieve in their life. Most people can tell you where they wish they could live, what kind of car they would like to drive, who they would like to go out with, the kind of person they would like to marry, where they would like to take their vacation, and the kind of career they hope to have. But, how does this do anything for anybody?

For most, life is a very selfish process. For most, each person sets about voicing what they think about what they think about. For most, each person sets about achieving what they hope to achieve. But, how does that help anyone?

If you are not on the path of consciously doing things that help people, animals, the environment, and the world as a whole all you are is a selfish, thoughtless creature. All you are doing is taking but not giving.

Ask yourself, who have you saved? Who are you saving? Who will you save tomorrow and the next day? If you do not have an answer to those questions, what does that say about you as a human being? How does that describe who you truly are?

You can help other life. You can save lives. But if you don't change the focus of your life from you, the only person you focus on is you. Focusing on you is a very egotistical state of mind.

Stop thinking about what you think. Stop thinking about you. Stop caring only about what you want. Stop spending all your time only attempting to achieve what you hope to achieve. Stop it and care. Stop it and do something to save someone. Stop it and take on the responsibility of saving someone. Do this and everything becomes better.

One small act of goodness can set an entire avalanche of goodness into motion.

Who are you going to save today?

* * *
23/Nov/2020 05:23 PM

How old do you have to be to not be young anymore?

Making Movies on Your Phone
23/Nov/2020 02:15 PM

I am really an advocate of making movies on your phone. The technology in most phones on the market today is far superior to what was used for Super 8 and 16mm filmmaking of the past. Plus, you have on-board audio. You no longer have to record your dialogue on tape and sync it to your film.

I know, I know… I'm from the old school where we used to shoot on film. Some people still do but the numbers have decreased. Way back in the way back when I said in some interview that once some high-end film is made on video the perception of video filmmaking will completely change and this has come to pass.

I also used to say, way back in the way back when, once they find a way to attach a microphone to the smartphone, smartphone cinematography and smartphone filmmaking will sweep the independent film industry. This too has come to pass. I can now attach a full on Sennheiser microphone to my phone when I want to get great audio. Plus, it's really easy to do.

Every phone is different so I would detail it here. But, look it up, you can do it too.

Mostly, I don't use a Sennheiser ME66 or ME67 for my iPhone filmed cinematography, however. I have a little Shure microphone that plugs straight into my iPhone, that I keep close at hand, that really increases the perfection of the audio if I want to do that. There's a few other similar mics out there which also provide truly increased audio quality. And, they're relatively cheap!

With the dawning of the video age, indie filmmaking became more affordable. This was drastically increased with the dawning of the digital age a few years later. Prosumer video cameras were fairly cheap and you could do some great things with them.

There were a certain group of people in the industry who gravitated towards DSLR cameras but I have spoken about this in the past… Yes, you can film movies with them but that is not what they were actually designed for. Thus, they have a certain lacking in comparison to an actual video camera. But, I won't go into all of the technical aspects of that right now.

Smart phones, particularly iPhones, have far surpassed all the cinematic excellence that one used to have to spend a lot of money to achieve. Meaning, anybody can now become a filmmaker. There are no more excuses!

All you have to do is to remember not shoot your footage up and down like so many people do. Turn your phones sideways. That is movie mode. That is fill the screen of your TV or theater screen mode.

A smart phone is all you need. Get out there and make your movie. It can be short, it can be long; it doesn't matter. Just get out there and do it! There are no more excuses. Your key to becoming a filmmaker is already right in your pocket.

All Going to the Lost and Forgotten
23/Nov/2020 09:37 AM

Think about a time in the long ago and the far-far away when you were young. If you were living the average life of a young person you probably had magazines and posters of the things of your era. Maybe you had a poster of a sport's personality, a singer, a band, or a movie that you liked on your wall. Me, growing up in the sixties and the seventies, at various stages, I had psychedelic posters on my wall. I had a poster of Peter Fonda riding his chopper in Easy Rider, as that was a very influential movie to me—I really loved that poster. As time when on and I got a bit older and more involved in Eastern Spirituality, I had pictures of Swami Satchidananda and Swami Sivananda around me. We each had our own thing. The people that we admired and the things that guided us. Where are all those magazine, pictures, and posters now? Where are all the posters you had on your wall? What happened to them? What happened to you?

We all grow up. We each evolve. We move forward in our life and we become what we become. For many/most, we never rise to the level of that something worthy of a poster on a wall they we hoped to become but nonetheless we each have hopefully lived our life as best as we can. You did what you did defined by your particular set of circumstances.

But, what about the back then? What about the evolution you hoped to embrace? What about the influences and the people who influenced you? What about the posters on your wall? What became of those people? Did they remain who they were in your mind? Or, like most, did they disintegrate from the role of idol to just another Joe, embracing the problems of life that we all face?

The thing about life is that there is the projected reality and then there is the reality of reality. As long as a person is a poster on the wall, they are no more than a picture. There are no feelings, there are no life-actions, there are no mistakes. They can't hurt you.

Think about the people that you have photographs of. Think about the people that you have taken photographs with. Where are those people? What happened to those people? What happened to those photographs? For some/for many, if you were in a relationship with a person, and the relationship faded away, you probably threw those photographs away. I remember this one girl I was going out with in my twenties, she was way into me, but I was only so-so into her. Initially, she pulled me into all of her family photographs and made me stand next to her, even though I didn't really want to be in the photo, whenever we went to one of her family functions. Then, I so amusingly remember the point when she pushed me out of a family photo, telling me I couldn't be in it. She finally realized the relationship was doomed. This made me smile then as it makes me smile as I remember it now.

Photographs lock you into a moment. They are a memory—perhaps a found memory but that moment is gone. What happened to all those photographs of you/of a time gone past if that person no longer liked you? What happens to those photographs when you pass on to the next life?

Every now and then I will find a whole group of family photos in an album, a shoebox, or a slide tray at a thrift store. Obviously, someone passed away and those who remained cared not about those photographs/those memories. Thus, they donated them. And, think about all of the photos that were just thrown in the garbage. Those photos once meant something to someone but no more. Who wants someone else's memories?

It's really scary how meaningless all of the things that matter so much to us, matter so little to anyone else.

…Even me, I've thrown away photographs and later realize what a big mistake that was.

So, here we are, our childhood gone. What happened to those illustrations of our youth; those posters on our wall?

What will happen to all of the photographs of you and all of the photographs you have taken? Found memories to us but meaningless to everyone else.

* * *
23/Nov/2020 08:44 AM

The reason most people don't accomplish anything with their life is that they don't know what they are looking for.

The Arrogant and the Ignorant
23/Nov/2020 07:14 AM

We are about to enter into another Lock Down here in Los Angeles due to the surging cases of coronavirus. What is the cause of this? The cause of this is the behavior of people and their believing that they are either immune, that it is all a hoax, or that they just don't give a fuck about their fellow human beings. But, people are getting sick and people are dying. Why? Because people are not taking this China-born disease seriously.

I was in an antique store over the weekend. There were people walking around who had their masks pulled down to chin level not covering their mouth and nose. Sure, they wore them to get in the store but as soon as they were out of sight of the staff, down came the masks, exposing others to disease. Masks are not solely worn to keep you safe from others; they are worn to keep others safe from you!

Last evening I was in the supermarket. My lady was standing next to me as I was picking out some broccoli for dinner. This old guy walks up right between us grabbing for those plastic bags that are on those rolls above the vegetables that you can put your produce in. I couldn't believe it. There are stay six feet apart signs everywhere but there he was right next to us grabbing for the bags. I voiced, *"What an asshole."* But, what am I going to do, kick his ass?

Over the weekend there was a big protest in Orange County. They were burning masks, protesting the recent COVID curfew, and the like. Nobody was social distancing or wearing masks.

People are dying! The current rate has just gone up in the U.S. to one person dying every sixty-seconds from COVID-19. Yeah, there is now some better treatments and the release of the vaccine is on the horizon but, due to the arrogant, due to the ignorant, and due to the selfish behavior think how many businesses are again going to be put in peril, equaling people's lives being destroyed, as this new Lock Down takes effect all do to people thinking only about themselves and not others.

Who do you think about when you do the things you do? Do you think about the other person or do you only think about you: what you feel and what you believe? If you only think about you then, by that very self-definition, you are a selfish person. If you are responsible for one person getting sick or one person dying what do you think that will do to your karma for the rest of your life? What do you think that will do to your ultimate life definition and evolution?

There is only one thing that anybody should be doing in life, now during this age of coronavirus or at any other time, and that is taking the other person into consideration—thinking about the other person first.

Care… Because if you don't, you have the potential to destroy the lives of other people. Care… Because if you don't, no one will care about you.

* * *
23/Nov/2020 07:13 AM

Why do most doors open in instead of opening out?

Step Back in Time
21/Nov/2020 07:47 AM

For each of us there are those memories that are very prominent in our mind. The first time you did something. When that very special something happened. Even when that negative something occurred. Those things were big. Thus, they are vividly remembered.

Then, there are those other things. Small things. No big deal events. Yet, for some reason, every now and then, they come to your mind. Not once but repeatedly. Why?

Here's the exercise for the day. Bring one of those memories into focus. One of those memories you periodically remember but they were just a passing moment of your life.

Think back ten years. If you're an old guy like me, think back twenty, thirty, or forty years deep. Look for one of those memories that continually comes to mind.

Once you have isolated that memory, calm your mind. Let your random racing thoughts dissipate. Truly focus on that event. Remember it exactly. Take your mind back in time and really feel the event. Do things like remember what lead up to the event. Think and find the words that were spoken. Go deeply into that memory and experience the feelings that you were feeling. Truly explore and relive that moment in your mind.

What will come from this exercise will be a bit different for each person. But, it will truly allow you to see who you were back then, what you were thinking, and what you were feeling. From this, you may come to a new conclusion of where and why you have arrived where you have in your life. How what you were feeling then lead you to what you are feeling now. Perhaps, you may even find an unrevealed clue as to why that memory has stayed in your mind—why it comes to your mind periodically. You may even learn that the passing event means much more to your life and your life's evolution than you initially thought that it did.

Step back in time and you may learn a lot about yourself and why you have ended up where you have ended up.

The People That Help You
20/Nov/2020 01:22 PM

There are some people that come into our lives and they truly help us. Whether this is accomplished by being our friend, giving us a ride when we need one, helping us move, helping us paint our house, onto people who we never met but have inspired or guided us through their writings, their actions, their whatever... For all of us, there are some people that have come into our lives that have truly helped us in large or in small amounts.

As we pass through life, not all of our relationships last forever. Sometimes people move away, sometimes people become busy with their families or new friends, sometimes people just drift apart. That's not a bad thing. That's just the reality of life. But, if a person has helped us they always deserve a place in our hearts even if we never see them again.

I think we can all agree that we really appreciate the people who have helped us in our lives whether we personally know them or not. This is why I forever advocate telling people, *"Thank you,"* whenever you can. Whether it is for a small action like picking up something you dropped, a server carrying your meal to your table, onto the bigger things of which the list is endless. *"Thank you,"* is one of the best things you can say to a person. Reach out; let people know that they have helped you. Tell them, *"Thank you."*

Some people, including myself, really set about on a course of consciously trying to help other people. This is not just for people I know. I try to do things that may help people I will never meet. Certainly, helping someone is not based solely in physical action. It can also be accomplished by saying nice things about a person, stopping or interrupting people from saying or doing negative things. Helping can come in all shapes and sizes but it has to be done. Helping requires you to do something.

Helping does not have to be done close to home. It does not only need to be provided to people you know. Look around the world, watch the news, read the newspaper, there are people who need help everywhere. If no one provides it for them they may be trapped into a negative life environment forever. But, if someone/if you cares enough to help, then their everything can become better.

There is a lot of negativity in this world. I imagine it has forever been like that in different shapes and forms. Some people believe helping is helping someone do something negative be this via word or physical actions. But, if anyone is hurt, that is never helping. That is only hurting. Everyone is a person. They all have feelings. They all have their families and their lived ones. No one deserves to be hurt. Thus, hurting is never helping.

So, what are you going to do today to help someone? What are you going to physically do, say, or write that helps someone? If you don't do anything, nothing is done. Thus, no help was provided.

Help begins with you choosing to help. It begins with you doing the right thing.

Care; care about the all and the everyone—even the people you don't know. Help someone today. Help someone right now. Help someone every chance you get and the world becomes such a better place.

* * *

20/Nov/2020 01:18 PM

If what you say is wrong then it is wrong.

Yet, think about the world. Think about how many people are saying things without ever researching the true facts. Think about how may people say things based upon their opinion and present it as fact even though what they are saying is not the truth.

Is a false fact ever the truth?

If what you are saying is false, what does that make you?

Answer: A liar.

Isn't silence a better alternative?

* * *

20/Nov/2020 07:19 AM

Do you remember when you made your first mistake?

Stalking
19/Nov/2020 01:15 PM

"If I wasn't already paranoid, I would become paranoid." That's the joke I told my lady today when I returned home from the supermarket…

A kind of weird thing has been going on in that for the second time in about a week a person has come up to me at my local supermarket saying, *"Scott??? I think I know you."* In both cases it was a female—a different female, I believe. Right now, in the age of coronavirus, with everyone wearing a mask, it's kind of hard to tell. But, if someone knows you they follow that statement up with something to the affect, *"I was in one of your movies. I took a class you taught. I met you at that art gallery opening, I used to be a barista at Starbucks, I like that book you wrote, or I'm a fan of Roller Blade Seven."* But, in both of these cases, nada…

I always remember when I would bump into the famed actor: two-time Clint Eastwood co-star and James Bond villain, Don Stroud. *"Hey Scott, it's me, Don Stroud."* I always knew who he was as he was one of my childhood idols. I thought, how humble is that guy? A famed actor and believing he has to remind people who he is.

But, in both of the aforementioned supermarket situations, nothing… They just finished up with, *"You could be his twin."*

Me… I, of course, refrain from answering questions or revealing anything about myself in situations such as these as you really don't know who you are talking to (or why).

Obviously, something weird is going on. And, unless I'm sleep walking and living some entirely different life that I don't remember in the morning or it's one of those cross-dimensional things where Scott Shaw from a different dimension is crossing over into this one, someone is stalking me for some reason. Or, maybe I have a doppelgänger. Two of me; that's scary! If I want to be really paranoid, maybe someone is impersonating me. But, why would anyone do that?

Stalkers are always weird. I mean they exist out there in the shadows and who knows why they do what they do.

As it has become easy to find the whereabouts of pretty much anybody these days, I guess this kind of stuff goes on all the time. You can't hide from that demon, cyber tracking, listing everyone's everything, internet.

I've had a few stalkers in my days. That's the weird think about being almost famous, people want to get to know you; either from a positive or a negative perspective. And, as I have long said, *"Everybody wants something from me but no one ever gives me anything."* So???

The people who just want to be friends are one thing but then there are the people who seek something else... Back in the days when I was writing a lot of articles for marital art magazines, (of which pretty much none are left), I got a few of those weird, macho people tracking me down and trying to start a fight. But, that's just not what I'm about. That's not what the true marital arts are about!

When I was living at this other place, maybe twenty years deep, whenever I would park my car on the street something went wrong with it the next time I drove it. If I parked it inside, all was fine. But, outside… Somebody was obviously doing something to it, but why? What did it prove? Though I do believe I know who it was…

Then, there was this one guy who wanted me to give him a role in one of my films. Every time I would go into this one shop he would magically show up. Obviously he knew someone who worked there and they would alert him when I arrived. I always thought that was funny. Eventually I gave him a part in a film. Amazingly, when I went into the shop after that he never magically appeared.

I've had a few online stalkers over the years. Maybe they would write bad reviews about my books or my movies or talk shit about me on message boards. But, to what end? What did it prove? Like I always say, everything you do has the potential to affect the life of someone else for years to come; maybe even forever… And, if you say or do something that negatively affects someone/anyone it will all come back at you. You did it. You did it to hurt someone. Do you believe there are no cosmic life repercussions? People always wonder why negative shit finds them and they don't succeed in what they hoped to achieve. Look in the mirror.

You know, the thing about stalking, especially someone like me, is what is the point? I'm a very approachable sort of person. Hit me up on Facebook if you want an answer to a question or just to chat.

Back in the day, when I was teaching a lot of classes and seminars, people would come and take a class if they wanted to know what I was about. But now, in a world of on-line everything, I just don't have the inspiration to teach via that method.

Some people send me an e-mail or something and they immediately want to meet fact-to-face. Then, they get mad when I turn them down. It's nothing personal. I'm just a fairly reclusive person. From experience, I don't trust people. It takes time for me to get to know someone. But, that doesn't mean that you have to stalk me. In fact, I'm a really boring person, why do you want to meet me at all?

But people, you don't have to stalk me! If you see me on the street or at a café or at the supermarket or wherever, come up and say, *"Hi."* Tell me who you are. Tell me what I can do for you. Or, what you can do for me. It doesn't have to be weird. You don't have to stalk me!

If You Need an Explanation You Don't Understand Art
19/Nov/2020 07:35 AM

  As someone who has been involved in the creation of art, in one form or another, for most of my life, I have throughout the years been confronted with the fact that people question what I am doing. Combine this with being closely associated with other artists and it seems that the paradigm is the same; some people understand art as being art and others question the why.

  In terms of art forms like writing: poetry, novels, and the like; and yes, writing is an art form, the inquiries are less obvious. A person likes the words, likes the style or they do not and that is that. But, as soon as you step into the other, more visual, realms of art: drawing, painting, photography, or film, then the questions become more obvious. But why? Aren't the visual realms of reality the most obvious? Aren't they the ones where a visual something is created? It is there. Yes, you can like it or not like it but its reality is true and pure onto itself. Yet, this is where so many questions arise. I cannot tell you how many times I have encountered someone looking for something when the fact of the obvious is right in front of his or her eyes.

  From my own personal perspective, I have encountered people questioning a photograph I took. Why does anyone want or need an explanation of a photograph? The image is right it front of your eyes. It is what it is. It is what it is in its purest form. Sure, you may like the image—sure, you may dislike the image but the image is what the image is.

  In many ways this is the same with paintings. An artist has a vision in their mind; they attempt to place it on canvas. Maybe they like it, maybe you like, maybe neither of you like it. But, it is what it is. Why is there any need for an explanation?

Film is the same. The filmmaker creates a conglomeration of moving images, ties them together, and creates a film of whatever length. It portrays what the filmmaker could capture and it is true and pure onto itself. The filmmaker may like it, the people who took part in the production may like it, the viewer may like it or they all may not. But, like and/or dislike is not the definition of art—creation is the definition of art. If it is envisioned, if it is created, if it is done, it is art. And, art is art.

I am sure we have all been to art galleries where people are having some long bogus discussion about they whys and the wherefores of an artist they did not personally know. They attempt to define that artist's reality not knowing the truth of their inner motivations. I am also sure we have each encountered people loving or hating an artist's work and their questioning the why of the artist's motivations.

If you need an explanation, you do not understand art. Art is art, it all stands on its own merit of creation. If it is create it is art. By this very fact, that should be explanation enough. Love it, hate it, want to own it, or discard it, that is all your personal choice. But, if you question the artist's why of the art, you do not understand art.

* * *
19/Nov/2020 07:33 AM

If you consciously do nothing you are walking towards Zen.

If you allow the dominating hands of life to keep you from doing something you are walking towards unfulfilled oblivion.

***

18/Nov/2020 06:56 AM

A fact of life is, once you've done something it can't be undone.

So, the question becomes, should you do something and suffer the consequences, be they positive or negative, or should you do nothing and encounter no consequences?

* * *
17/Nov/2020 03:55 PM

Sometimes the only way you can realize your mistakes is when you back over time and analyze how your actions caused you to not achieve what you hoped you would achieve.

* * *

17/Nov/2020 12:33 PM

If you charge a fee for what you do, you are a business person.

If you do what you do for free then you are a benefactor.

A business person takes.

A benefactor gives.

Never confuse the two.

* * *
17/Nov/2020 12:32 PM

It's easy to pray to god asking for what you want but what are you actually doing for the betterment of anybody's anything?

Hawk
17/Nov/2020 10:05 AM

Last week I looked out onto my patio and I noticed that there was a hawk sitting on the railing. Wow! *"How cool,"* I thought. Then it flew off.

A bit later in the week I was taking a walk around a nearby park with my lady. We saw a hawk sitting on the ground. We both pulled out our phones to take a photo. Before either of us could, the hawk took off. The only thing was, in his claws he was holding a just killed squirrel. Okay, that's weird...

Whether it was the same hawk or not, I don't know. There's a lot of hawks that fly around my section of the outbound greater Los Angeles area. Though, of course, that is all nature—the hawk killing the squirrel and all that. But, it just seems so heartless—so predatory. I mean, I like squirrels.

Recently, there was this squirrel that was making a pattern out of coming to eat his lunch on my patio. One of my neighbors was apparently feeding him peanuts but he did not want to eat where he was fed. He was even trying to bury his treats in my planters. Though I felt very bad doing it, I had to shew him away as I did not want him and my cats getting into it. But, I certainly wanted him to be happy and not dead.

Again, I don't know if that was the same squirrel. Probably not. But, the loss of all/any life is sad.

When I did the movie, *The Roller Blade Seven,* Donald G. Jackson came up with the name Hawk for my character. I never really questioned why. I just used it. It was just my character's name.

No big deal one way or the other… But, here/now this is the first time I questioned it. I don't feel very predatory at all. In fact, I feel just the opposite.

Nature is a weird thing. The strong over power the weak but it always seems that the strong come at the position from a place of power. The hawk knew he could grab, kill, and eat that squirrel. He didn't go after a Pit Bull or a German Shepard.

And, that's the thing about life, the predatory are always the lowest on the spectrum of pure consciousness; they do what they do from an expected position of power. Power that someone else or something else gave them. They attack the weak or at least the weaker but they never go after the more power-full because then they would loss.

I don't know… Nature is nature but we humans possess a choice, a choice that we really need to make. A choice to hurt no one and no thing no matter what.

* * *
17/Nov/2020 09:45 AM

You are never going to be the person you were yesterday.

* * *

17/Nov/2020 09:44 AM

If you have to tell somebody you have something that means you really don't have it.

* * *

16/Nov/2020 02:35 PM

If right now is the best you can ever be where will you be?

* * *
16/Nov/2020 01:29 PM

When have you done enough?

*   *   *
16/Nov/2020 01:05 PM

Everybody is looking for someone but is anyone looking for you?

*   *   *
16/Nov/2020 01:05 PM

If you broadcast to the world that you can fight there will always be someone who will want you to prove it.

The Reexplaining of Reality
16/Nov/2020 08:25 AM

Your life is based on the way you understand reality. Your life is based on how you define your interpersonal relationship. Your life is defined by the way in which you act and react towards others. Your life is based on the way you interpret the way other people have treated you.

Throughout your life you have interpersonal relationships with people. The way they treat you comes define the elements of how you feel about people, the way you trust or do not trust people, and the way you act and/or react to other people in future relationships. In other words, you learn by experience. How someone treats you, what they do to you or for you, sets the stage in how you will analyze, chart, and gage the next and the next and the next person in your life.

How a person treats you has the potential to define how you will judge all other people because we all learn from experience. If your personal interactions are positive, then you will come to view all (or at least most) people from a positive perspective. If your interactions are negative, then you have the potential to, more than likely, see other people through an untrusting eye.

One of the main things to remember in this process, however, is that it is all based on your interpretation. How you have interpreted the actions of others is how you define that experience and how you define others. But, your definition is not necessarily the truth. It is simply your definition. It is how you have judged and how you have interpreted what that someone else did or said to you. But, the fact is, you do not truly know what was in their mind. You do not truly know why they did what they did or said what they said. All you have—all you are working off of is what you think but what you think is all in your head, it is not in their head, so you may be completely wrong.

For example, I had an interesting reinterpretation of a situation that happened to me many-many years ago. I don't know why this situation came to mind but it did.

The story is, a friend of mine literately insisted that I meet him in a city several hundred miles away from L.A., up along the Eastern Sierras, as his stepson, someone I had trained extensively in long-distance bike racing, was doing a race. I didn't really want to go. But, my friend insisted. Due to our long years of friendship, I gave in.

I had a new girlfriend at the time, so instead of taking my vintage Porsche, whose heater didn't work, we decided to take her car. Though the car was new, it broke down. I had it towed to the city where we were to meet my friend hoping to find a mechanic who could fix it. As it was a small town, there were none. When we arrived at the motel, I explained the situation to my friend and his ultimate words to me were, *"Sorry, but this is my only vacation…"* He left us stranded.

Though those words basically ended our friendship, as I believed they were beyond selfish, I always took them at face value. The other day, when the incident popped into my mind, this weird realization came over.

To go back in time a little bit… This guy forever attempted to mess up any relationship I was in. He would always talk trash about the girls I was with and coax me to go out and hang out with him instead of them. As time when on, he met this older woman, who was just two years younger than his mother. She had two kids, they became a couple, got married, and had their own kid. But, he never really changed how he reacted to me and my relationships. I would occasionally bring girls over for Sunday dinner, every now and then, and the like, but he forever maintained his negative appraisal of all of them. Where all of this came from, who knows??? We all have our inner programing and our unknown reason's why. But, what I realized about the aforementioned situation, where the car broke down, was that what he really wanted was for me to go off with him, his wife, and his stepson and leave my girlfriend behind. After replaying his words, I realized that was his motivation. After all of our years of friendship, he was asking me to choose him over choosing her. But, that is not just the kind of person I am. I would never leave anyone stranded and alone.

So, was what he did simply seeking attention and hoping that his best friend would choose him over her? Yeah, maybe… But, it was all in the presentation.

Now, there can be all kinds of debate about his psychological makeup and what motivated him to behave in this manner in the first place. He, like I, had a really fucked up childhood leading to a not very well-balance adulthood. But, all that we have when dealing and interacting with other people is what is presented to us. Then, it is only us, who comes up with a definition. But, all a definition is, is our interpretation of what took place—what someone else did to us, and how we feel about that doing. Is that definition the truth? No, it is only our interpretation.

So, think about it… …When someone does something to you and you think you know why; think again. Because you can never truly know what is in someone's mind.

China Rules the World
13/Nov/2020 07:30 AM

Ever since the beginning of the COVID-19 Coronavirus Pandemic I have question, *"Why is no one mad at China?"* Here in the U.S. people are mad at our politicians. Some are mad because the politicians are making people wear masks. Others are mad because the politicians have shut down businesses in hopes of keeping the virus from spreading. Others are mad at the politicians because they believe that they have not done enough and perhaps they have become sick or one of their family members has died. But, none of this is the fault of the politicians in the U.S. They are just trying to figure things out as best as they can. It is the fault of China! But, where is the focused anger on China? They are the ones, who due to their unsanitary condition in a wet market, exposed the entire world to this disease.

There is no one in this world that has not been affected by the COVID-19 Coronavirus. For some, it has been small. For others, it is has been much larger. People have lost their jobs. People have lost their businesses. People have lost their health. Many, across the globe, have died. And, we will never know the true number of deaths for in places like India (and China) the true numbers are not even calculated and revealed. Plus, this pandemic is nowhere close to being over. More devastation, destruction, and death is to come.

According to the news today, one American dies every forty-three seconds from COVID-19. We didn't create this disease—it was not formulated in the United States. Yet, our people are dying from it, as are people across the globe. Why is no one mad at China? Why is no one taking China to task for having taken control over the entire world?

We are told that a vaccine is soon to be released. But, what will be the impact and the cost of that vaccine to the human body and to life on the whole? No one knows! It is all just speculation. Plus, keep in mind, the promised vaccine is thought to be ninety percent effective that means that one in ten people can still contract the virus after they have received the vaccination.

Ever since I first traveled to China I knew that they would become the World Power. Why? Because they have a massive population that is scared to death of their government. They do what they are told and when they don't, look out. Even with some of the integration of New Culture and enchased person wealth that has been somewhat adopted since the 1990s in China, the essence of the people are the same. They operate from a position of fear. Look at the people who have rebelled. What has happened to them?

As I have said in the past, if some country did this intentionally to the U.S., Europe, Russia, or wherever, it would have lead to war. But, no one has done anything. They have given China a pass. But, it is their fault! They have destroyed the lives and have killed many. No one has not been affected by COVID-19. Why can't the people who caught the disease, why can't the people who lost loved ones due to the disease, why can't the people who's lives were ruined by the disease sue China for compensation?

So, when you look around at the condition of your life—the way you are currently living your life, remember who is to blame. It is not your politicians; they are trying the best that they can.

This is the fault of China. China is in control of the world. China rules the world. They are the ones that you should focus your anger upon.

Confrontation in the Rear View
12/Nov/2020 02:11 PM

  It truly struck me as strange this morning when I headed out on the streets. There was nobody there. The streets were virtually empty. It was kind of like at the beginning of the pandemic when no one was driving anywhere. Very strange and unexpected, especially for a city like L.A.

  I did my drive across the city, did what I had to do, and was on my way in the direction of home. I was pulling up to this stop light and out of nowhere this mini van cuts me off and pulls right in front of me just as the light was turning red. I threw my arms up in the air. Plus, they did this for no reason. They had their own lane going straight as they were obviously planning to do. Me, they cut off my right turn and I had to wait for the light to change for them to move forward. Not cool, but whatever…

  What happened next is the point to all this… They flipped me off as they drove away. What! I mean, *"Fuck you!"* You did something wrong, you cut me off, and now you're flipping me off.

  As someone who sometimes suffers from that, *"You can take the boy out of the jungle but you can't take the jungle out of the boy syndrome,"* what they did kind of pushed me in the wrong direction. Maybe I was just too hyped after drinking my Starbucks Venti Flat White Latte? I don't know? But, it's all kind of how a situation is presented to you, you know. I mean, we all, every now and then, do that stupid thing when we are driving. But, when you do, you give the other driver that wave of, *"Sorry,"* and move on. But, flip me off. It really hit me the wrong way.

Now, this kind of nonsense goes on all the time. I have watched it throughout my life. Someone is at fault—someone does something wrong or maybe they just want to take control over a situation and attempt to employee some sense of over-empowerment in a nothing situation, so they lash out. But, in few cases people who do that would do what they did to a person's face. They only flip people off in their rear view mirror. Same with the internet. Everyone OUT THERE is oh so powerful. They can say anything they want from their keyboard but what about face-to-face?

This situation just struck me the wrong way, I rolled down my window and gave them a big, *"Fuck you."* Lost in that moment I was hoping that they would say something. But, as could be expected, they did not.

You see, this is where the birth of negative situations takes place. Someone does something unthinking or simply wrong. They do it, they are the one who made a mistake, yet they blame it on the person they presented the mistake to. Things can really escalate out of these moments to something very negative. I have see it many times and have lived it a few.

The good thing, if you want to call it that, is I catch myself in these moments, knowing that whatever would occur would not end to anyone's true benefit.

You know, in some ways, that's the problem with being Scott Shaw. …With being someone Almost Famous. Or, maybe better put, someone who used to be Almost Famous… In the Almost Famous position of life, people come at you. They hope to make a name for themselves by doing so. Then, when and if you kick their ass, they call the police with the, *"Whoa is me,"* defense and they want to sue you. And, the problem with the Almost Famous tag is, you don't have the people network or the big money of the Truly Famous to back you up. So, it just becomes a stupid street fight all based on someone doing something which was actually meaningless to you.

You know, I remember this one time, I think he was a stalker cause I saw his truck a few times, but, I was driving down the street, (well, actually up a hill), and this guy pulled right up next to me. He had those really dark tinted windows, so I couldn't really see what he was doing, but I guess he didn't know that. Every now and then the light would hit just right and he was driving while nonstop flipping me off and he appeared to be screaming at me. Get a life dude, get some control. But, then I turned right, going to my intended location, and he just drove on. I saw him drive by me a week or two later, there he was flipping me off again. Why? I have no idea. I certainly didn't know him.

And, that's the thing—that's the essence of the evolving trend of anger and violence and why stupidly flipping someone off equals nothing good but it can end in something very bad.

For someone like me, who literally fights most everyday, in martial art training, you get a different understanding of person-to-person reality and you see how foolish physical combat can be. Someone wins, someone loses, but who cares?

I see so many martial art instructors making the same training mistake that people from the first generation of American martial arts, like myself, made. They do things like wear weight belts on their ankles when they kick or on their wrists when they punch. They believe that doing this helps to develop strength and power but all it ultimately does is destroy your body. Ask any orthopedist. Ask anyone, like me, who also used to do it. Because ultimately, what is the point of having that super-superior punch or kick? Life and even the martial arts is not a never-ending combat zone. We are not living in a zombie apocalypse. In fact, by studying the martial arts you should gain the understanding that you never need to fight. What the martial arts basically comes down to is an enhanced understanding of physical—person-to-person reality. Can you kick someone's ass—do you have a better chance of kicking someone's ass? Sure, maybe. But, so what… If you do, then what? Then you get arrested. Then you get sued.

So, what does this all tell us? It tells us, if someone flips you off—if they flip you off even if they were the one at fault, don't let them and their actions control your reality because a reality based in anger and violence leads to nothing good. Smile and drive on.

From Here to Wherever
12/Nov/2020 07:34 AM

I was watching, *From Here to Eternity* last night. It's a really good movie that really stands the test of time. The one thing that I particularly noticed was that everyone was smoking and drinking whiskey all the time and then they were locking lips. That must have been really nasty. I mean kissing someone who has just smoked is really foul; add to that whiskey and…

I grew up in a household of parents who smoked. It was at a time when they were really announcing how bad smoking was. My father had his first heart attack and the doctor told him to quit. He said, *"I like smoking."* His next heart attack killed him. He was only forty-eight.

A bit later in life, when I was maybe thirteen, my friend's father asked me if I smoked. I did not. I never did. But, my mother's smoke was so all over the everything that my clothing smelled of it. Then, add to that all of my years upon years of involvement in the Korean martial arts, where everyone of my Korean instructors and contemporaries smoked. And, it was everywhere. My father-in-law, (my last drinking buddy), died from lung cancer from smoking. Believe me when I tell you that is not a good way to go out. Add to that all of the seedy bars I hung out at in Asia and forget about it…

In the 1970s and into the 1980s I would meet a pretty girl and one thing would lead to another. You know how it goes… The problem being, many of them smoked. Kissing someone who smokes is just nasty. I'm sure I have written poems about that published somewhere? Yet, a man needs his women...

I remember I had this one semi long-term girlfriend when I was in my twenties. She smoked when I first met her. She supposedly quit for me. I had left her West Hollywood, just above the Sunset Strip and the *Whiskey A-Go-Go,* apartment to go somewhere but I had forgotten something. I ran back up the stairs, went inside, and there she was smoking. She had lied. She still smoked. She was just hiding it from me. Addiction is a hard-core thing.

I have this one friend that I have known forever and ever. We came up through the days of Punk together. But, I knew him long before that. He started smoking at the late age of thirty and he still smokes to this day. I never understood why. He's a smart guy. Plus, he is in complete denial about the reality of second hand smoke???

Think about life. Think about the things that you do. Think about how the what you do does something to someone else. How much do you care? Do you care at all or are you willing to fight for your right to party?

From Here to Eternity; great movie. But, more than that it is a depiction of a time, a place in history, that offers a unique view into interpersonal reality. It also offers a unique view into how people behave. How do you behave? How do the people you know behave? And, how do you define your life by what you choose to do, what your doing does to others, and how what you do affects the greater whole of the world? Are you willing to die a horrible death and maybe kill others in the process just so you can do something that is really a nasty habit. ...Think about it... Not just smoking but what do you do that is offensive and hurtful to others.

If you hurt yourself—if you hurt anyone, you are hurting the entire world.

*　　*　　*
11/Nov/2020 02:27 PM

How many things in your life are a secret?

* * *
11/Nov/2020 09:33 AM

Forgive the flaws.

* * *
11/Nov/2020 08:26 AM

Right now STOP. Don't think.

Let it last as long as it will last.

Push the Reset Button
11/Nov/2020 07:29 AM

For each of us there is something in our lives that we wish that we could change. For some, this is something large like move to a new city, get a better job, buy a new car, get a divorce from a husband or a wife, or find a pathway away from loneliness. For others, it is something small like lose some weight, learn how to play the guitar or learn a new language. What that something is can never be actualized, however, unless it is brought into reality and it is for this reason that many people never rise to the level of self fulfillment, contentment, and life accomplishment that they hope to find. If you want to do something, if you hope to change something, that will never happen unless you do it.

Life is a complicated array of desire verse actuality. Life is lived by availability. Though most everyone wishes that they could raise themselves to that level of greatness that so few have found, that may not be possible. But, what is possible is for you to define what is lacking in your life, delineate what you wish your life would be, and then take steps towards achieving that end goal. If you don't try it will never happen.

I was in a thrift store the other day looking through the vinyl. This girl comes up and starts chatting me up about music, old record stores, and the like. At one point she pulls down her mask. (As we are in the midst of the COVID-19 coronavirus we are all required to wear masks). She exclaims, *"This is what I look like."* She was, what I would consider, a cute thirty-something white girl. Then, her phone rings. *"I've got to get this."* She answers, *"Yes baby, yes baby, I'm leaving right now..."* She bolts for the door without saying another word to me. I'm guessing her boyfriend was waiting for her in the car outside and she had stayed in the store for what he deemed to be too long. You could her the fear in her voice as she replied to him. She was clearly looking for a new man in her life. Obviously, I was not that person. But, if you don't try…

This is the thing, we all want that something else, that something better—we hope to be better, we want to be more… As stated, for some, that something else is something big—it is a big change. For many, that change involves people—bringing other/new people into our lives.

People are complicated. They each have their own set of desires and they each have their own demons. They too want what they want. If you fall into their net of desire then you may walk with them for a time or a lifetime. But be wary, each person brings with them their own pattern of behavior and aspirations and, as with you, once you have lived what you lived; you may want to leave it behind. So, few people can truly be counted on to give you what you want forever.

Your life is your pathway. Your life is your passageway to achieving what you want. What you have done and what you are now doing does not have to be the forever definition of your life. But, if you want something different you must decide to take the steps to make that something else—that something better become a part of your life. It is you who must do it. It is you who must make it a reality.

Push the reset button.

Fuck You Pig
10/Nov/2020 02:34 PM

So… I was going over to this one shop I like off of Pacific Coast Highway today. As I was driving up I noticed that there was a cop talking to someone who has set up a tent right in the middle of the sidewalk on the side street that runs along the side of the shop. I parked in their parking lot, that's behind the store, and was headed for the front door of the shop. I had no choice but to pass by the cop, a person kneeled down next to the tent, and, as I later realized, there was someone inside of the tent.

As I got closer I could hear this girl yelling, *"Fuck you, Pig! Fuck you, Pig,"* from inside of the tent. Obviously, the cop was asking this couple to leave.

Now, there's a lot of levels to this tale. I mean, I don't know… I don't think it would be that comfortable sitting on the cement inside of a tent. I mean, there's no padding or anything like that. Plus, why would you want to be just off of a busy street like PCH? I would think setting up your camp in a park or something like that would be way better.

Here in L.A., and I am sure in a lot of other cities, the homeless problem has really gotten out of control. I mean, there are encampments all over the place. And, they are dirty. You know the old saying, *"Never shit in your own back yard?"* But, that is exactly what they do. I have known and/or witnessed a few business owners who have really been hurt by the homeless moving in—especially in this time of the pandemic.

There has been a lot of upheaval in recent months. Some cities, like L.A., have actually decreased the budget of the police department massively. The Powers That Be recently cut their budget by one hundred and fifty-million dollars. From my point of view, this is not a good idea as the world is going crazy and you need the police to keep order.

The other part of the issue is that there is so much scrutiny now being placed on police officers that they can't do their job. I mean, back in my day, if I had been screaming, *"Fuck you, Pig,"* to the face of a police officers I would have gotten a baton smacked up side my head.

Anyway, so I went in the shop and when I came back out, I noticed the tent was still there. They male part of the couple was now sitting behind it smoking a cigarette. Between the tent and him I literally had to walk out in the street to get around them. They had completely taken over the sidewalk. I noticed the girl who was inside the tent was now sketching in a notebook. The cop, long gone. So, I don't know what he did or did not do or what he told them to do? What I do know is that there is now a tent in the middle of the sidewalk just off of Pacific Coast Highway.

The world right now is really messed up. Cops are not being allowed to do their job. I get it… The world is changing… People are attempting to invoke a cultural change. But, without order what do we have? We have anarchy. But, anarchy is not a good thing. Look at all the recent riots. What has occurred from them? Damage, loss, and pain. Even look at the off the grid communities that people have attempted to set up in cities like Portland; what occurred? Damage, injury, and violence again other people. Recently, they have been closing the CVS stores in San Francisco. A few weeks ago I saw on the news how homeless people were just walking into the stores and taking whatever they wanted. They did this with the news cameras on them and they did not even care because they knew the law would do nothing. If you don't have order, what do you have? If you don't have order and respect for other people what you have is homeless people deciding that they can plant their tent anywhere they want and all of the rest of us be damned. We can walk out in the street if we want to get around them.

Selfishness and uncaringness towards other people is never the pathway towards anything good or better.

Principles of the Precepts
AKA Good Behavior Verses Bad Behavior
10/Nov/2020 09:43 AM

I believe we have all encountered situations where we are interacting with someone, on a personal level, and they do something that we find very offensive. Whether it is something as small as coughing or sneezing without covering their mouth onto eating in a very unrefined manner onto saying rude or hurtful things in the presences of other people onto doing something that is truly verbally or physically unacceptable. But, look around, it happens all the time. Maybe you do it. Maybe other people judge you as being less than all-right.

Certainly, this is a time in American politics where tempers have been flaring and people have been doing less than refined things. Some applaud this behavior. Some despise it. But, it still all boils down to one person doing one thing that someone else finds offensive.

It's not only here in the U.S. Look around the world; things are going crazy in a lot of places. Belarus is in political turmoil. Thailand is currently in a state of massive protest. Hong Kong, forget about it... ...Interesting how the COVID-19 Coronavirus emerged out my China when they were having all of those protest problems with Hong Kong. The pandemic put those massive protests to bed immediately and now the restrictive laws the Chinese government hoped to pass are all in place. The Arab Spring took place a couple of years ago causing massive upheavals. But, all this is nothing new. It goes on all the time. Here or there on the national scale or on the person-to-person personal scale, people do things that other people consider to be not right. People get offended and people get hurt. Why? Because someone is doing something that someone else considers wrong.

I got a chance to catch a few minutes of a documentary shot in Tibet last night. Interesting, the video footage was all so clear. The guy apparently just left Lhasa and traveled deep into Tibet documenting his interactions with the people and his experiences. He did this until the Chinese forces caught him in some restricted zone and they threw him out of the country. This too happened to me too back in the mid-1980s. I only wish that I had the photo and video technology that is available today back then. Me, I had this camera bag with three very heavy 35mm cameras and several lenses over my shoulder. If only I had a smart phone back then I could have captured so much more of my experiences in such a more projectable manner.

Again, here was a guy, doing what he was doing; hurting no one. I found the documentary very interesting, as I am sure many other people did, as well. But, the Chinese government found it offensive. They kicked him out. At least they didn't take his film as they did with me. …Me, back then, they put me on a bus and shipped me to the boarder where I had to find my own way back to civilization. Not fun! Offensive! But, the powers that be found me, and my presence, offensive. So, who is right and who is wrong?

I think, if we look to the world outside of us, we all know what is considered to be right and considered to be wrong. We all know what we consider to be right and wrong. Yet, think about it, how many times have you done something that you would consider wrong if someone else had done it? Whether it is sneezing without covering your mouth, stealing something, lying, hurting someone and not caring, whatever... You did it, yet if someone else did it or did it to you, you would find it very offensive.

As I often say, all life begins with you. It is you who chooses to do what you do. What do you choose to do? And, are you consciously in control of yourself enough to care about not offending or hurting that other person; whoever that other person may be?

All life begins with you. It begins with what you do and what you do in the presence of others. What do you do? And, do you care? Do you think about how what you are doing is going to affect that someone else who may not like what you are doing? Or, do you only think about yourself? ...Do you not think about anything or anyone before you do what you do?

Life can be a good place. But, that goodness all begins with what you say and what you do. It all begins with how you react.

So, what are you going to do? What are you going to do that may offend someone else? And, what are you going to do if you do offend someone else? Your life, your choice. But remember, what you do can begin as something very small and move outwards to affecting the whole world.

Good or bad, positive or negative, it all begins with what you do. What are you going to do and why are you going to do it?

*   *   *
09/Nov/2020 07:16 AM

If you drink alcohol-based drinks and you stop drinking alcohol-based drinks your body and your mind will truly change.

If you drink colas and soft drinks and you stop drinking colas and soft drinks your body and your mind will truly change.

If you drink coffees and teas and you stop drinking coffees and teas your body and your mind will truly change.

If your drink water and you stop drinking water you will die.

Liquid is required for life to live. The purer the liquid you drink the purer your body and your mind.

You can alter your body and your mind via what you drink but if you do it takes you away from the pureness of your true spirit and being who and what you were truly meant to be.

How You Remember a Memory
08/Nov/2020 02:54 PM

I was flipping channels last night and *The Rock n' Roll Hall of Fame Ceremony* was on HBO. I've never been a super big fan of that yearly presentation but I get how *The Rock n' Roll Hall of Fame* severs its purpose.

It was kind of weird this year as due to the 2020 pandemic and all the repercussions there was no actual ceremony so everything was just taped presentations of famous people talking about their thoughts and remembrances of the bands and then the recipients coming on, via tape, making a few jokes, and saying, *"Thanks."* Though I didn't spend too much watching the show, I did happen to pop back just when they were doing the bit on T. Rex. It really made me think about the fact that Marc Bolan had died decades ago and the young people of today probably don't even know who or what T. Rex was and/or their place in rock n' roll history. …Meaning, what purpose does *The Rock n' Roll Hall of Fame* serve when it's only a memory churner for old folks?

Me, I was a big fan of T. Rex. As a young adolescent I was really into the whole Glitter Rock thing. Alice Cooper, Mott the Hoople, the New York Dolls, and T. Rex were always blasting from my stereo in the early 70s.

I was actually lucky enough to see T. Rex live. I'm sure I've told this story somewhere before but when I was like thirteen T. Rex was playing at the Santa Monica Civic Auditorium. None of my friends wanted to go. I was always counter-culture orientate, most of them, at that time, were not. I didn't have a ticket or anything but I got on the bus and took it to Santa Monica in the early afternoon. I walked over to the auditorium hoping to get a ticket, as I knew the show was sold out. Luckily, this group of people had an extra ticket. They had arrived early hoping to sell it. They sold it to me and asked me if I wanted some acid. *"Sure."* They threw in a hit of Orange Sunshine, that normally sold for about $2.00 back then, for free. They went their way, I went mine. I dropped the acid and walked around the Santa Monica shopping area waiting for the show, which was set to begin in a couple of hours.

I went back to auditorium, tripping of course, near the time the show was to begin and found that the seat they had sold me was great. It was right up there front and center to the stage. The people who sold me the ticket showed up a few minutes later, also tripping, and we were set to go.

I forget the opening act, but T. Rex eventually came on and the band was great. The thing was, it was a time in history when everybody was getting high, so everyone was sitting around smoking weed, passing around joints, and the like, and the energy of the crowd was just not very up. In some ways, I felt sorry for Marc Bolan as he was getting upset, and verbalizing it, that no one was really getting into the music, him smashing his Les Paul, and the like. I mean it must be hard to watch your career diminish right in front of your eyes. He hadn't had a hit song in some time and everyone was just too stoned to really get into what he was offering. But, in my mind, he always held an important place in the music of my life and I still enjoying listening to T. Rex from time to time.

After the show, my new friends asked me where I was going, as they had a car, but they were going the opposite direction so I walked back up to Wilshire Blvd. and took the bus back to Hollywood with my ears massively ringing. Rock shows were very-very loud back then. Especially being in the front row. Don't do that to your ears people or you'll end up like me with tinnitus.

Today, I was listening to the news on the radio, and as we just had a presidential election last week, the reporter was discussing how California was considering going solely to mail-in ballots in future elections. The problem, as she said in her own words was that, *"Young people don't understand signatures or know where the post office is."* What! Who doesn't know how to write their signature? Who doesn't know or can't figure out where the local post office is?

Times change. The reality of life changes. People die. New people are born creating new generations and new types and styles of everything. It ALL always changes. Even the people whose music was an influence on us, it only means what it means to us. Really, all we have is the life we live and the memories that living generates.

What I remember is what I remember; you could care less about it. Just as what you remember is what you remember. I did not live it; so I can listen to your remembrances but what you lived will never truly affect my life.

The Rock n' Roll Hall of Fame is just a memory churner for someone who liked a band way back when. Everything like that is nothing more than a creation for someone who wants to remember what was but is no more.

So, don't get lost in the past—not even your own past. Because if all you are doing is remembering what it was like way back when, you

will never allow yourself to live what it is now—
now, no matter how old you are.

* * *

08/Nov/2020 07:14 AM

Why do people hope to associate with successful people?

Because they want something they haven't got.

Why do people seek to associate with spiritual teachers?

Because they want to know something they don't know.

Every motivating factor in life is based upon desire—getting something you don't have.

What happens if you want nothing?

*   *   *
07/Nov/2020 02:05 PM

If you present yourself as living by a higher standard you must live up to that higher standard or you become nothing more than a hypocrite.

* * *

06/Nov/2020 07:13 AM

Ready, Set, Go!

Let you hair grow and stop shaving.

Men and women both.

Let your naturalness flow.

Why not?

Fixing the Broken Glass
AKA Developing the Taste for Blood
05/Nov/2020 09:38 AM

You have a glass. It is a very functional glass. You can put it under the faucet and get a drink of water anytime you need one. Maybe it's even pretty. Maybe you really like it. One day you drop it. It breaks. It's gone. You can try to glue it back together but, even if you can, (which you probably can't), it will never be the same. It's perfection and functionality are gone forever. Now what?

That was your glass. When you broke it you may feel very bad about it but it was your fault. You can blame no one else. It is you who must strive to replace it. But, what about if someone else broke that glass? …That glass that you really liked and was very functional. Then what? What if they don't care about your glass, you getting a drink of water, or you? What about if they broke that glass intentionally? What about if they broke it and they just don't care?

Recently, here In the U.S., there have been a lot of protests taking place. There are various motivations for these protests but the one thing that has become one of the primary components for these protests is that certain people take them to the next level and decide to rob, loot, and destroy the businesses and the property of other people. In fact, as has been well documented, there is a certain subset of these so-called protestors who arrive simply to loot and pillage. Do they care about a cause? Do they care about those they are hurting? Do they care about the fact that they are destroying the livelihood of some other person? No, most probably not. They have simply developed the taste for blood and they have found that by arriving at a protest they will most likely be able to get some of their desired possession for free. Is that right? No, it is not. I am sure all of the people who read this blog will agree. Yet, it is going on all over the place. And, this style of behavior is not isolated to these recent protests. It takes place via various forms and various methods all over the place all of the time.

The other day a news reporter made an interesting statement. She said, in essence, *"I think everyone who breaks in and loots one of these businesses should have to go back and help the people they have robbed reconstruct their life."* Think about it… That would be a very eye opening punishment if these criminals would have to do that. As she said, *"It would cause them to see that they are people too."*

Think about your own life. Think about the people that you have robbed from, hurt, or damaged in some way, shape, or form. Have you ever been forced or simply desired to step in and replace what you have broken? Have you ever even cared enough to think about doing something like that? Or, are you like most; you live in a world of blame, denial, and excuses?

Here's the assignment—the assignment if you are mindful enough to take it on; go out there and fix what you have broken. Step back into the life of someone you have hurt, stolen from, or damaged, and glue his or her drinking glass back together.

Do this, and the entire world becomes a better place.

New Ideas
05/Nov/2020 06:59 AM

Where do your new ideas come from?

Do you ever spend any time cultivating new ideas?

For some, new ideas pop into their brain all the time. For others, new ideas are far and few between. What is the cause of this? It is the person's own fault?

Life is a pathway of newness. Every day is new and different. Yes, for many of us, we may encounter similar things day in and day out but there is uniqueness is all things life. The same can be very different. You simply have to look for the differences. Do you?

This is the same with inspiration. Are you seeking new and insightful inspiration? Are you looking for that new revelation?

Many people lock themselves into sameness. Some do this from a very negative life perspective while others just give up. In either case, no new newness is found. It is not found, as it is not allowed to enter the mind.

For others, they encounter life with their eyes and their mind open. They hope to see new things. They want to experience new insight. It is a choice.

A choice is what sets the foundations for you allowing new ideas to come to your mind. …Your choice to open up and let them in.

New ideas and inspiration can come from anywhere—they can be instigated by virtually anything or any life experience. You simply have to be open to them.

So, here's the exercise: STOP, sit quietly, close your eyes, look into your mind, what do you see? What is there? Don't judge. Simply experience. What do you see when you look into your mind? Define it.

Once you have done that part of the exercise, question, what do you want to experience in your mind? Know what you are seeking. Everyone wants some type of inspiration. Everyone's is different. What is yours?

At this point stop attempting to demand it. Just sit quietly for a time and let it naturally come to your mind. Don't judge, don't control, simply allow new ideas to come to your mind.

Some of these new ideas you may like. Some you may not like. But, never hate yourself for allow them to come to your mind because from them you may gain new insight into who you truly are and what is the true definition of your life but they may also creatively inspire you to take the next step in the evolution of your life.

Inspiration and new ideas can come to you at any time, at any place. You simply have to be open minded enough to allow them in. Then, it must be you, who takes the initiative to put them into play.

If you allow inspiration to be an integral part of your life, new ideas—new inspiration will come to you all the time. Consciously allow this to occur.

Life is always new. Life is forever changing. Allow yourself to become a part of this process and new inspiration(s) will forever be your guide.

Don't turn off the inspiration.

Penance
04/Nov/2020 03:59 PM

Penance: Voluntary self-punishment inflicted as an outward expression of repentance for having done wrong.

How much of your life do you spend performing penance? How much of your life do you even contemplate doing something to yourself when you understand that you have done something wrong? In fact, do you ever even contemplate how you can self-correct and/or self-discipline yourself when you have done something wrong or hurtful to someone else? Do you ever even care when you have done something that is considered to be wrong or hurtful or are you so locked into the mindset of selfishness that you never even contemplate the fact that you may have done something wrong?

We all know what is right, just as we all know what is wrong. Killing, stealing, physically hurting someone else, cheating, lying, even saying hurtful things are all wrong. And, there is many more. We all know what things are wrong. But, look around you; wrong goes on all the time. Do you do it? Do you applaud those who do?

All problems with the world begin with you. Just as all problems with the world can be fixed by you. The problem with the problem is, nobody cares about that other person. Nobody cares as long as they are getting what they want, doing what they want, and saying what they want. This is the sourcepoint of all that is wrong with the world. People do not care about the other person. They do not care about their own wrongness. And, they certainly do nothing to correct their wrongs, nor do they possess enough self-awareness to punish themselves when they do something wrong.

When we are children, it is quite common for our parents to step in and unleash some form of punishment when they believe we have done something wrong. Certainly, civilized society has its definitions of rights and wrongs and when a person crosses the line, and are caught doing it, they are punished according to societal laws. But, these are all forced punishments. They are not the individual caring enough about any damage they may have created to actually chastise themselves and perhaps do something to personally reprimand themselves.

Take a moment right now; think about something that you did that you know was wrong. Maybe in the moment you were not thinking about anyone else and did not care about the affect your actions would have on that someone else, but right now, look to one or more of your hurtful actions; bring it clearly into your mind, focus on it. What was it? Who or what did it hurt? Don't be denial-filled in this exercise, truly chart out what you did. Now, if you had been caught for doing this deed what would your parents, your friends, your society have done to you? Even if it wasn't something that broke the law, what would someone else have done to you, to reprimand you, if they could?

Most people never think about any of this. They just think about what they think about—they want what they want, they do what they do, and the all and the everybody else can be damned. But, is that the kind of person you really want to be? Do you really want to be someone who does not care about or take responsibility for your negative actions or words. Do you want to live your entire life emanating from a space of lying or making excuses for what you have done?

People get hurt. People get hurt by what other people do. That, in itself, is the definition of wrong. And, there is always the instigator. The person who initially did that something that hurt that someone else. Is that you? Is that who you want to be?

Now that you've thought a little a bit about the hurt or the anguish you may have caused, what are you going to do about it? Are you going to be big enough to try to correct your actions or are you simply going to continue to live in denial? Are you going to perform penance?

Life is a pathway of action. Everyday you make a choice to do what you do. If that choice involves forcefully taking from or hurting someone else, then what does that make you? If you are not willing to view your actions of hurt and damage as wrong, again, what does that make you?

All pain and all pleasure begin with what one person conceives and then what they put into action. What have you put into action? Who have you hurt? What have you harmed? What are you going to do about that?

If you are a true person, you attempt to fix any damage that you have caused. Are you are true person? Are you whole enough to perform penance? Or, do you just live your life in a state of uncaring denial, seeking justifications and making excuses to yourself and to everyone else for you have done that is wrong?

All life begins with you. What are you going to do next?

Round and Round and Round and Round
03/Nov/2020 09:38 AM

I always find life to be this interesting production of movement from one place to the next but the next is always intertwined with the before. You bump into people you used to know, a new person you meets knows someone who you used to associate with, and people, years later, proclaim the same patterns of action that someone else has created in your years gone past.

Back in 1990, I was ask to create this documentary about doctors who traveled to China to perform eye surgery to needy patients for free. If you feel like it, you can view element of the handheld camera work I did for the film on my YouTube Channel. As for the full-on, high-end footage and film, I have no idea what became of it???

Just a side note I flashed up… One of the funny things that occurred when we first arrived at the hospitable was that the doctor, who had traveled from the U.S., always referred to me as, *"Doctor."* Inside the O.R., the head surgeon of the hospitable hearing this immediately handed me a set of scrubs and expected me to go in and perform surgery. *"I'm not that kind of doctor,"* I laughingly exclaimed… Anyway…

One of the things I have noticed about life is that due to the extensive amount of writing I have done, and books I have had published, people always seem to want me to help them write their own tale of woe. And, due to the extensive amount of films I have created, people who have written their life's tale, hope that I can help them turn it into a film. I get asked for this assistance all the time but it is really not what I do. I don't make that kind of movie and I really don't care that much about any of these people's life—at least not the to degree that I would want to help them write their autobiography. Plus, they never want to offer me big bucks to entice my interest.

The reason I mention this is that this other western doctor, who had arrived to help with the eye surgeries, had written an autobiography or something. It was unpublished, of course. He lived somewhere else, outside of California. I forget where. He hoped I could turn it into a film. But, why would I do that? How is his tale so much more interesting than anyone else's?

After I returned from China I would get call after call, fax after fax (Fax—remember those?) from him with hopes that I would help him out. I never responded. Finally they stopped.

Now, let's look thirty years later; today… Recently, one of the local nurses who I met back then got in touch with me via Facebook. We've exchanged niceties and all of that kind of stuff. Today, I just got the ask—the ask to help her write her life story and turn it into a movie. This made me smile. Like I always say, it seems everybody wants something from me but no one ever give me anything.

Here I am, (again), another person asking the same ask. But, like the various character's I portray in my Zen Films frequently questions, *"What's in it for me?"*

Here we all are; life… We live what we live. We all have a tale to tell. Some are better than others. Some feel theirs should be told. Some are more humble and just keep it to themselves. But, in all of the living, in all of the asking, where is the giving? Where is the focus? On yourself or on the someone else?

I always find that the people who want to tell their tale have some sort of strange ego. For it is them, and generally only them, who wants to tell their tale. But, what about the other person? They too have lived a life.

So, the world goes round and round and round and round. We all live our lives as best as we can. But, what we live always comes back around. What we live, we live again and again and again. The same experience(s), via a different person at a different time. What does it all means, I don't know? But, think about it, think about your own life; isn't what I am saying true? You live what you live what you live and then you live it again. You live it, maybe you want to tell others about it, but it is truly only you who can understanding the interworking's—the inside out of your existence. So, telling people about it, do they really care or do they only care if it somehow affects them?

Mindfulness
02/Nov/2020 01:10 PM

Mindfulness, or as I like to spell it out, Mind Fullness is one of the essential elements of causing your body and your mind to rise to a level of enhanced awareness, self actualization, and, dare I say, enlightenment. But, how many people even contemplate mindfulness as they pass through their day? How many people take note of any element of how they are feeling or how they are experiencing life unless they are thrown into a moment a chaos by spraining their ankle, having something stolen, or experiencing someone breaking their heart? Then, the experience is all about them. It is all about feeling what they are feeling. But, is that mindfulness? No. That is simply being forced into encountering an emotion. Mindfulness occurs from a much more pure and focus state of mind.

When you are washing your hands do you contemplate the temperature of the water? Sure, if it is very cold or very hot you are forced to think about it. But, what about when it is lukewarm? …When it is just average? …When it is the way you always expect it to be? Do you experience the water, how it feels on your hands, how the soap feels and smells? Do you ever contemplate any of this? Probably not. Few people do. But, here lies the source of the problem of why so few people understand the concept of mindfulness.

In traditions like the martial arts, one is taught to train the body and their mind and bring them into an acute harmony so that they can exactly perform physical techniques. Yes, this is a style of enhanced physical and mental training that few people truly embrace. For most martial artists, however, they never transcend beyond the physicality of the martial arts. They are happy and proud to demonstrate how well they can perform a technique or how many boards they can break. But, this is nothing more than exhibitionism. For all of the martial artists out there, ask yourself, how often did your instructor teach you how to truly encounter your moment both in terms of internal feelings and external stimuli? For most, the answer is never. Why? Because the instructors were never taught nor did they seek out the pathway to true mindfulness.

Mindfulness is you truly experiencing your moment. Wherever you are, whatever it is you are doing, it is you allowing your being to truly feel all that is around you and then stepping deeply within yourself and coming to terms with how you are an interactive part of the entire process.

In Tantra Yoga, one is taught to truly embrace their partner while engaged in an intimate relationship. Whereas most people enter into these occurrences via desire and seeking that good feeling that arises from a sexual encounter, the Tantra Yogi is taught how train their body and their mind to step beyond the physicality of the act itself and, by truly moving deeply it the transcendence of the act by truly merging with the experience via the partner, they can gain a glimpse of Satori. Again, how many people follow this pathway? How many people even ponder following the pathway of Tantra? Very few.

Is mindfulness a complicated process? Yes and no. The true answer is, no. It is extremely easy to allow yourself to become consciously mindful of all of the things that you do. You just have to do it. The problem is, very few people have ever trained their mind to become mindful. They are just taught to do what they do until they are on to doing the next thing. Sure, they may love or they may hate what they are doing. Sure, what they are doing may make them feel good or feel bad. But, none of that is mindfulness. That's simply responding to stimuli. Mindfulness is choosing to become aware of all that you are doing, all that is being done to you, removing your process of thoughts and definitions and transcending to the essence of the experience. It is there that a true understanding of life—your life may be encountered.

Right now, STOP, take a moment, shut off your thoughts, emotions, judgments, and predetermined notions. STOP and feel. STOP and experience. What are you feeling? What does your life experience feel like? How does your body feel? How are your emotions feeling? What are they causing you to feel?

Take some time and feel what you are feeling. Take some time to come to terms with why you are feeling what you are feeling. Take some time and analyze how what you are doing, what you did, is causing other people to feel.

Feel, experience, transcend. Find where you are and why. Meet mindfulness.

* * *

02/Nov/2020 09:12 AM

If a person is charging you for the techniques they are teaching you they are a businessperson and you are their boss.

If a person reveals their knowledge to you for free they understand the authentic nature of knowledge and from them you can learn the true essence of awareness.

* * *

02/Nov/2020 06:42 AM

If a person is trying to make themselves appear to be something more they are not helping you to become a better person or the world to become a better place as they are only focused on themselves.

* * *
31/Oct/2020 02:06 PM

Wouldn't you rather listen to some really good music than listen to someone brag about themselves or tell you how you should live your life?

*   *   *

31/Oct/2020 12:17 PM

The difference between prayer and meditation is that in prayer you are asking for something, in meditation you are seeking the absolute nothing.

* * *
30/Oct/2020 10:13 AM

The people who talk the loudest are generally the least accomplished.

* * *

29/Oct/2020 12:55 PM

How many mistakes have you made?

How many of the mistakes that you've made do you remember?

How many of the mistakes that you've made do other people remember?

How many of the mistakes you've made do you lie about?

How many of the mistakes you've made affected other people?

How many of the mistakes you've made have you tried to remedy?

Your life is defined in part by the mistakes that you've made and what you've done after you made the mistake.

* * *
29/Oct/2020 07:54 AM

What would you rather have hanging on your wall and have to look at day after day, a diploma or a work of art?

How Well Do You Do What You Do?
28/Oct/2020 09:04 AM

How well do you what you do? How much do you practice at becoming the best you can be at whatever it is you want to be?

For example, in the martial arts we practice the same technique over and over and over again in order to become as proficient at it as possible. There are forms where a prescribed set of techniques are performed in a specified order so that the practitioner can gain mastery of body and mind coordination and exacting physical movement.

In music, the musician practices relentlessly in order to become as proficient as possible. They practice scales, listening development, and hand coordination techniques all with the hopes of mastering their musical instrument.

Like the martial arts, the dancer practices the techniques of the movement of the dance over and over and over again. They attempt to find perfection in their physical movement.

For the artist, they study the movement of color. They work on their sketching skills. They lay paint onto the canvas time after time after time. Many times they do not like what they have created but they realize to raise themselves to the perfection of art—to truly embrace art, this is the pathway they must follow; painting and painting again until they develop and master their own unique style.

How much time do you spend developing the ability to become the best you can be at what you want to be?

For many, (for most), they do nothing. Yes, yes, pretty much everybody wants to be something but most do nothing to achieve it. They have their dreams and maybe they give what they hope to become a half-hearted tried. But, they never do what it takes to become a master of whatever it is they hope to become. How about you? What do you do to become what you truly hope to become?

Here's the assignment for the day… What can you actually do today to bring yourself closer to becoming what you truly hope to become? Define it and then do it. Spend today growing closer to what you hope to be.

The secret, if you can do it today, you can also do it tomorrow.

Spend the time, make the effort to becoming what you truly hope to become.

* * *

28/Oct/2020 08:59 AM

Someday they'll be a cure for everything, then what?

* * *
27/Oct/2020 01:58 PM

How often do you try to understand things from the other person's point of view?

The Projection of What You Expect
27/Oct/2020 09:12 AM

Undoubtedly, the primary condition that causes the demise of most relationships is the projection of expectations. A person wants someone to be some way, to behave in some manner, to do things in a certain way, but that person will not or cannot. Thus, end of the relationship.

People commonly project their expectations onto all things outside of themselves. They constantly think and talk about what they think someone else will do. But, how can they know? Each person is a highly unique entity and what he or she thinks, equaling what he or she does, may change at any moment. Just because someone thought or did something yesterday does not mean that they are still willing or will do it today. Yet, think about most people's lives, think about how much your own life is based upon what you expect other people to do in both a positive or negative manner.

Most people never take the time to chart their own thought process. They think what they think, causing them to do what they do, but they never find the source of that pattern of thought leading to that implementation of expectations. How about you? Do you know why you think what you are thinking, leading to what you are expecting from someone else and why? Or, as is the case with most, do you just think, do you define others; do you create your expectations for others based upon some undefined something that you know not what?

Why do you expect someone to behave in a certain pattern? The answer to that question is twofold: first of all you are basing your predetermination upon what you believe they have done in the past. But, how do you know anything about anybody? Sure, you may have heard, you may have read, you may have even witnessed, but again, what a person did yesterday does not necessarily define what they will do today. Some people actually evolve. The second causation for expectation is desire; what you want from a person and how you want to receive it. Think about any relationship you have been in: be it personal, professional, causal, or intimate. What was that relationship based upon? It was based upon your expectations being met. But, who are you to expect anything? Who is anyone? By expecting something from someone, by expecting them to behave and do things in a certain manner, aren't you robbing that person's ability to be a true example of what is truly inside of them?

The moment you have expectation you are projecting your own reality onto someone else. The moment you voice your expectations you are removing the element of free choice from that someone else.

How many times has someone been cast to being something they are not via someone else's expectations? How many times have other people believed a falsehood about a person due to someone voicing their expectations about a person?

If you think, voice, or actualize your expectations about another person, you are robbing that other person of being and becoming who they truly are. Stop it! Let each person be who and what they truly are. Stop expressing what you expect someone else to say or do. Stop forcing them into becoming what you want them to be. Stop it, and then each person of the entire world is allowed to be the perfect example of themselves.

* * *
26/Oct/2020 10:17 AM

What is good?

* * *
26/Oct/2020 10:16 AM

Lying to yourself does not mean that you are not still telling a lie.

* * *
26/Oct/2020 10:13 AM

Just because you have earned credentials in a field of knowledge does not mean that you have become the all-knowing purveyor of righteous wisdom.

* * *

26/Oct/2020 08:19 AM

How much of your reality is a projection of the truth and how much of your reality is a projection of the way you believe things to be?

*   *   *
26/Oct/2020 08:19 AM

You can believe anything that you want to believe but just because you believe something does not make it the truth.

* * *
23/Oct/2020 09:12 PM

If anyone believes that an enlightened person does not have to deal with the realities of life they truly misunderstand the concept.

The Curse of the Course
22/Oct/2020 09:29 AM

Someone posted a photo quote from Russell Brand on Facebook the other day that I found very revealing, *"Cannabis isn't a gateway drug. Alcohol isn't a gateway drug. Nicotine isn't a gateway drug. Caffeine isn't a gateway drug. Trauma is the gateway. Childhood abuse is the gateway. Molestation is the gateway. Neglect is the gateway. Drug abuse, violent behavior, hyper sexuality and self-harm are often the symptoms (not the cause) of much bigger issues. And it often stems from a childhood filled with trauma, absent parents, and an abusive family. But most people are too busy laughing at the homeless and drug addicts to realize that your own children could be in their shoes in 15 years. Communicate, Empathize, Rehabilitate."*

Though Brand is mostly known as an actor and comedian he is also one of those people who actually tries to make things better. Whether you like his style of presentation or not, he is one of the few individuals who became awakened via his own traumas and downfalls and used his experiences to guide his life towards the realms of raising human consciousness, helping people heal, and making the world a better place. Few people can claim that. Can you?

Think about the people you know. Think about the life that you have lead. Think about what other people have done to you: whether intentionally or not. Think about what you have done to other people. Has what other people have done to you made you a better or a worse person? Did it cause you to become a good person or a bad person? Once you became either a good or a bad person, how did that cause you to do things to the life of others? Do you ever ponder any of this? Do you ever think before you do: act and react?

Other people are the primary cause of the creation of all of us. How we were treated as a child, how we were treated as an adult; all of these actions combined lead us to what we have become. What have you become? Are you a good vehicle for life? Have you made someone else's life better or have you caused damaged to them? Do you ever ponder any of this? Do you even care?

Here lies the problem with human beings; they generally only think about themselves. They only heap praise and help onto those they like or those they hope to gain something from. And, then they hurt others. Why do they hurt others, commonly due to the negative things that were done to them by other people.

The fact of life is, there is no cure for bad behavior. It is not like we can push a button and everyone will become nice, do good things, and never hurt anyone. People, by their very nature, are a selfish breed. Thus, they act; they react to life based upon their experiences. If those experiences were negative, it is very common in a person repeating and echoing that behavior. They are doing onto others as has been done to them.

Think about a person in your life—a person that you truly know. Not just some acquaintance or some internet fantasy. ...Someone who you have nothing but good thoughts about and nothing but good things to say. Why is that? Is it because they were the perfect person and had no flaws? Probably not. But, maybe they helped you when you needed help, maybe they were their for you, maybe they were kind to you. But, the main ingredient is, most probably, they never did any bad thing(s) to you. Thus, they are held in a position of reverence in your mind.

Are you one of those people? Are you are person who does not hurt anyone? Are you a person who strives to help someone/everyone?

The basis for all things Good Life is a person who is honest with themselves. They do not lie, they do not justify, they do not deny. They live in a space of ever-expanding awareness where they learn from their faults, their mistakes, and they attempt to overcome any interpersonal damage that may have been done to them by others. Mostly, they strive to hurt or damage the life of No One.

How much time do you spend thinking about this? How much time to you spend bettering and healing yourself? How much time do you spend righting your wrongs? How much time do you spend making the life of other people better; asking for and expecting nothing in return?

We are all created by our experiences. We are all created by what others did to us. But, we can gain control over who we are to become and what we create in the lives of other people. You just have to take control over your mind and care enough to care. Care more about the other person than simply reacting and reanimating what someone else did to you.

Killing Loneliness with You
AKA Defensive Offensiveness
21/Oct/2020 02:30 PM

I have pretty much finished up all of my current projects so I was staring into a blank day. I don't really deal well with not having something to accomplish. I never have. Years ago my shrink told me I really needed to learn how to relax. Hasn't happened yet.

Due to the coronavirus thing, I can't go back to Japan. ...I can't really go anywhere. Thanks China! I'm waiting for this new electric sitar I had made for me in India to arrive. I'm planning to do this abstract raga thing with it. But, I can't get started on that until it gets here.

With nothing really to do, I decided to go and hit the L.A. cityscape. I jumped into my car and I pulled up the album *Dark Light* from the band *HIM* and cranked it up. It's a really good album. I hadn't listen to it in a while. That album came out in 2005 and probably heralded the band's pinnacle of commercial success, at least here in the U.S. Scary to think how long ago that was...

Anyway, listening to it sent me to thinking... I remember way back in the way back when, I was playing that album (on a CD—remember those?) and driving my lady and one of her friends somewhere. Her friend liked the music and inquired about the band. I told her it was *HIM.* *"What does that stand for,"* she asked. *"His Infernal Majesty,"* I replied. The woman was a devout Christian. She never spoke with my lady or me again. Then, as now, I think, how strange—how people allow something so small like the band someone listens to (and the band's name) to define who you do or do not let into your life. She liked the music… What changed?

Last night, I watched the new Guy Ritchie movie, *The Gentleman*. It's a very Guy Ritchie film. I guess that's a good thing; right? To have such a distinctive style of filmmaking that you come to be known by it. In one part of the film a character is referred to as, *"The Chinaman."* The minute I heard that, my first thought and words were, *"How Political Incorrect."* Nobody says that kind of stuff anymore—especially not in a film. A bit later, this one character is referred to as, *"A Black Cunt."* The actor calls out racism. Then, Colin Farrell, doing that great Cockney character he does, goes into a whole discourse about it isn't really racists as you are black and you are a cunt. Ritchie really pushed the PC boundaries in that film. I like it!

All that sent me to thinking about how everyone has become very sensitive about racial and other negative depictions. And, I get it. Times have changed. Many people, immediately, call up the fact that as I am White I don't understand. But, I do. I have said this before, but when I was young, few people in my grammar school referred to me by my name. They all called me, *"Honky,"* or *"White Paddy,"* as I was the only Caucasian kid in the school. But, I didn't let that define who I was.

All this caused me to I think back to the holiday's last year. My lady and I were at one of her cousin's houses doing that family sort of holiday thing. But first, I must go back in time…

The year before that, at the same house, I was sitting at a table discussing the curious case of eidetic memories and the fact I possess one with this person who has advanced degrees in psychology. She was detailing how in her practice she came upon several people who had eidetic memories and how they were each very-very different. Different people remember different things in different ways. For me, it's like I rewind a tape and can remember things exactly as they took place. It's really a curse. I remember everything. Anyway, this other family member sat down and got involved in the conversation—one of those people you really don't want involved but what can you do? She said she was going to test me next year. So, she told me the name of two of her yoga instructors and what day she took their classes. How stupid, I thought. Anyone can remember that. But, I thought/hoped she would just forget all that nonsense by the next year. She did not.

Back to last year's holiday get-together... She had her reminder set. She pulls out her phone, calls up the information, *"What did I ask you?"* I told her the names of her instructors and the days of the classes. I even reminded her that I asked if her male yoga instructor was hooking up with his students as that kind of behavior is very common in this modern era. All of a sudden, she said I was wrong even though she confirmed I told her the correct names and days. *"You're wrong! You're a liar! You can't remember anything!"* She literally screamed it. I don't know... Maybe she has some inner demons, maybe she is angry at her life situation, maybe she doesn't like me? Whatever... But, who behaves like that?

It was one of those times that if had I not been there with my lady, and had it not been her family, I would have gotten up and left. She was very rude. Rude, for no reason.

The evening drags on, we eat our dinner, I drink some wine, and the aforementioned woman's husband and I, and a couple other family member's, are standing around the center island of the kitchen. They were jokingly speaking of all things Korean-American and I made what I thought was a joke, *"Oh, you Orientals…" "I'm really offended by you saying Oriental,"* said the husband. His brother chimes in (thankfully), *"My wife says that all the time. It doesn't mean anything."* His wife is White.

So, here's the question, if you are close to someone, as I thought I was to these people, can you make a small joke about race as long as it is not mean spirited? They could have (and have) ripped on me for being White in the past. It's just a joke! I get it! But moreover, can a person not like what one person says but not also condemn their own wife (or whomever) when they literally scream something false at a person (another supposed family member) out of nowhere? Who draws the line? Where is the line?

Thinking of Koreans and Korea, I think to all of the Caucasian, African-American, and people of Middle-Eastern decent that revere Koreans and Korean martial art culture. What I suggest anyone/everyone do, if they are not of Korean descent, is to learn the Korean language and then go to Korea and see what the indigenous Koreans are actually thinking and saying about you. I mean, it is horrific. I cannot tell you how many times I have been in Korea and listened to people talk total shit about me. They obviously did not know that I speak Korean but that is all part and parcel of the Korean culture. They talk shit about everyone/anyone—especially if they are not Korean. But, just as when I was in grammar school and in other situations around the world, I do not let that define who I am.

Times are changing. I get it. But, in these changing times, are people simply looking for a reason to call out someone for something/anything? Are they looking for a reason to fight simply because of what is lacking inside of them? A person who is internally centered isn't defined by what someone else says about them—especially when it is a joke. But, if someone/anyone is defined by a lacking, an emptiness of self-empowerment, then they look for any reason they can find to condemn others.

As proven by the life I have lived, I am not a racist. As proven by the life I have lived, I am also a bit of a joker. I like to keep things light and happy. But, when someone turns happiness in something it is not. Who ultimately is to blame?

But, with all the thinking behind me, I stopped at a few thrift stores, (my drug of distraction). I got back in the car and listened to some more *HIM*...

"Memories, sharp as daggers pierce into the flesh of today. Suicide of love took away all that matters and buried the remains in an unmarked grave in your heart. With the venomous kiss you gave me I'm killing loneliness with you."

PS: I'll probably be skipping the family holiday extravaganza this year.

Can I Practice the Martial Arts Without Fighting?
20/Oct/2020 04:19 PM

"Can I practice the martial arts without fighting?" This is an interesting question I was asked the other day by a young person who was interested in studying the martial arts. The simply Zen-ness of the question put me in place of having so many answers and so many ways I could have answered. But, the simple answer is, *"Yes."*

To elaborate…

True martial arts are not solely about fighting. Yes, historically, they grew out of the need for warlike self-defense and solider-to-solider combat. But, as far back as their inception there were always those practitioners who saw them as something much more than simply learning how to fight. Throughout the centuries there have been those individuals who refined these arts and made them more about developing physical and mental self-awareness than simply about combat.

From my own perspective, I literally grew up practicing a Korean style of martial arts, Hapkido, from the age of six forward. And, though Hapkido is not considered a hard-style martial arts, it is very much about self-defense and overcoming the opponent. When I was in my early teenage years some of my friends were studying the Five-Animal System of Kung Fu from Ark Yuey Wong (rightfully known as the father of American Kung Fu) in Chinatown. Sometimes I would go to watch them train and, due to the kind nature of Ark Yuey Wong, he would stand me up and either he would or he would have one of instructors teach me some moves. They were very different from what I had previously been exposed to. And, though I questioned their combat effectiveness, I immediately understood their meditative nature.

A bit later, I was also exposed to Tai Chi Chuan. Again, though I understood this was a system based upon ancient forms of physical combat, it was not combat orientated and, instead, was moving its practitioner towards a more refined level of mental and physical awareness.

Though Hapkido was my first art, when I was about twelve I also began to train in Taekwondo. A fact that many people do not know about Taekwondo is that in the mid to late 1960s and into the 1970s there were a few Taekwondo orientated gymnasiums in South Korea that were intentionally designed to turn out Taekwondo instructors that could take the art across the globe.

In South Korea, a male is drafted into the army at approximately nineteen years of age. While in military service, many a South Korean male was first exposed to Taekwondo training. Once they finish their required primary and their reserve time, some decided to make Taekwondo a career. For those, they could go to one of the aforementioned training facilities, intensively train for a year, and emerge as a 4th dan black belt, which made them an instructor level practitioner. From there, many of these people found their way to other countries where they established Taekwondo schools. This is why as immigration requirements began to be less restrictive in the various Western countries around this same time, a large amount of South Korean practitioners relocated and opened Taekwondo schools of self-defense.

Taekwondo is a hard style system of self-defense. But, in its early stages there was much more to this art than simply sparring. It was a truly refined and precise system of self-defense where weapons, weapon forms, various Ki development exercises, and meditation were all taught. This is why so many of the early practitioners of this art, myself included, looked down on the later direction Taekwondo took when it began to focus solely on competition and it became the national, *"Sport,"* of South Korea.

The point I am making is that, even a hard style system of self-defense like Taekwondo, at least at the point of its inception, was much more than simply a system of fighting. Thus, all styles of the martial arts have the potential to be more than simply a fighting art form.

"Can I practice the martial arts without fighting?" Yes, you can. But, the devil is in the details… Most school owners are operating their schools as business. It is their livelihood. Thus, they must cater to the needs of the masses. Do most people want to learn how to meditate? Do most people want to learn how to perform a physical meditation? Do most people wish to use the techniques inherent in the martial arts to unify their body and their mind and to raise themselves to a higher plane of consciousness? No. They want to learn how to defend themselves. Maybe they even want to gain the pride that comes from rising through the various belt levels of the martial arts. Thus, the martial arts are not held back by tradition to be primarily fighting arts, they are held back by the teacher and the students.

So yes, you can find a martial art style where you do not have to fight. This is where personally motivated exploration comes into play. Will most school owners tell a perspective student they do not have to fight if the question is asked? Of course they will. They are a businessperson. They want to sign up as many students as possible. But, just like in all things life—just like in all undertakings, you have to look beneath the surface, you have to listen beyond the words, you must seek the essence and reveal why any person is saying what they are saying. If you want to know what you are actually getting into, look beyond the obvious. There you can find a style of martial arts where you never need to fight.

* * *
20/Oct/2020 11:35 AM

Just because somebody says they won't do something doesn't mean they actually won't do it.

The Projection of What You Haven't Got
20/Oct/2020 10:59 AM

It seems everybody sees the rich, the famous, and the accomplished as having the world by the tail. They view them as someone who has it all. For some, they view those people as an inspiration to work hard and climb their own ladder to success. For others, they despise them simply because of their success. But, what is the desire to be rich and successful motivated by and why are those who have achieved it both loved and hated?

First of all, everyone has their problems. No matter how rich, famous, or powerful a person becomes, they too have their own unique set of difficulties. They have their own obstacles. They have the things that upset them. They have the people that love them and they have the people that hurt them. For anyone who truly wishes to understand the reality of reality all they have to do is to sincerely peer into the life of a person who has risen to a high level of notoriety and they will quickly see that all things are not simply the way that a person from the outside projects them to be.

Here lies one of the key elements to understanding the cost of all forms of life. An individual in the public eye is projected to be *A Something by A Someone Else*. Whether what that other person sees them to be is true or false is almost irrelevant because that is the way that person perceives them to be, thus that is the definition they project to the world. But, is that projection a truth or it is simply a perception projected from a person who has no true understanding?

Think about your own life. Think about the people you have thought to be A Something.

Whether this person was your teacher, your boss, a politician, a sports, music, or movie star… You saw them as A Something. Your described them, in your own mind and to other people, as A Something. But, were you right or were you simply placing your own definition onto them based on your own preconceived misunderstanding? Did you ever question this fact before you created your definition?

People think what they think about someone else based upon their own frame of cognizance. But, how many people truly understand and/or investigate this fact before they come to their conclusion? How many people look deeply into themselves and the description of their own personality and reality (and how it came to be) before they cast a definition onto that someone else.

As I often say, people are a very selfish breed. Though this is a fact of life, it does not change the reality of that fact. Some people are simply more vocal or physical in their appraisals of others but that does not make their assessment of another person the truth. Thus, is born conflict. Conflict never leads to anything good.

When we look to very selfish people, when we look to very opinionated people, when we look to very abusive people, when we look to people who are very oblivious to other people's feelings, we see the same thing; these are people motivated by whatever it is that drives their brain. They think what they think, they say what they say, they do what they do, but all that they do is driven by some internal something—some internal something that no one else possesses. This is the birthplace of sociopathic behavior. A person who is solely focused on themselves and uses that trait to motivate their own selfish conduct that is damaging to the lives of others. But, think how many people behave like this all the time. They do what they do, they say what they say, defined only by their own internal stimuli. How about you? How often do you say or do things without taking the other person's life or feelings in consideration? How often do you do what you do motivated only by what you think about that someone else?

This brings us back to the point of projection. …Your projection about that someone else and how that projection causes you to act and to speak…

Before you define anybody else's anything, think about this, do you personally know that other person? Do you <u>truly</u> know that other person? If you do, then you may possess a certain understanding about their true inner motivations. If you do not know them deeply and personally, then you have no idea about what makes them do what they do, so how can you speak to their reality? If you do not personally know a person then you have absolutely no idea about who and what they truly are, so why should you be thinking about, speaking about, or acting based on what you think about them at all?

Life is a projected reality. It is your projected reality. You know you but how well do you know you? Have you ever truly travelled deeply into your mind and found out what motivates you to do the things you do? Have you ever truly explored penetratingly into your own psyche to find your hidden inner-reality and what caused you to be you? Very few people have. They all have a million excuses why not but without this exploration everyone just acts and defines others based upon nothing more that a undefined feeling that emanates from within them. But, if they don't know the motivating factors for that projected reality, how can anything they say or do be based upon fact?

The sage is silent. The louder a person speaks, it illustrates the less they truly know. The more a person endeavors to project their own reality, in an attempt to make it the definition of someone else's reality, the more clearly you can see that they are not a <u>true</u> person living life from a <u>true</u> space of knowledge. For the person who truly knows themselves, and actually comprehends human reality, they appreciate that they can only truly know themselves and from this they do not need to define themselves by and/or to project their own insecurities onto someone else no matter how well known that other person may or may not be, because Self is only Self and you can only truly know Your Self when you lose your desire to define Your Self in regard to other people and you realize that by attempting to cast your definition onto others this reveals how little you actually know about the truth of your own Personal Reality.

Be you. Know you. Because you can never truly know anyone else.

The Gift of Giving
but Who Gives What and Why?
19/Oct/2020 10:42 AM

As a fan of films, filmmaking, and filmmakers I am constantly on the lookout for that next great piece of cinema. Whether it cost millions upon millions of dollars or fifty cents to create when I see that piece of cinema that really moves me, it is a great experience. Even while viewing the films that aren't, what I consider to be that great, it is always an experience to watch them and contemplate what went into their creation.

As a filmmaker myself, I am always trying to explore new realms of possibilities in cinema. As I stopped producing character-driven movies a decade or so ago, for me it has become all about the visuals. Whether a film is character based or not, isn't that the case for all of us? When we view a film we want to see that special something that touches us in that certain kind of way.

As we all know, Netflix is a cinema powerhouse. The one thing that I notice whenever I am watching a Netflix film is that they are so elaborate. In fact, it looks like they give their filmmakers carte blanche to do whatever they want. As a film viewer, sometimes I see that a particular piece of cinema should really be cut down to a more refined product. But, that's just me. Netflix let's 'em run…

Having been involved in a Netflix production, when Adam Sadler and his team asked me to do a small bit in his film, *Sandy Wexler* a few years back, I personally saw the power that Netflix money commanded. At one point when I was on the set, they shut down Sunset Blvd., right in the middle of the Sunset Strip midday to get their shots. That is the power of money.

I think all filmmakers, myself included, would love to get a Netflix deal. I would love to make a film of the caliber they show on Netflix. While watching their films sometimes I say, *"Just give me a small portion of that budget and I could give you something great."* I say that as most of my films (my character driven pieces) cost like $300.00 to make.

But, the thing is, I have no way into Netflix. I have no way to pitch them a film. Though, with all of my years of no-budget filmmaking experience, I could give them a product at least as good as most of their films for a fraction of what they are paying to create their movies. But, that's the game. The game no one outside of the film industry understands. There is no way in unless someone invites you in. I can go out and make a million films on my own dime. I could, like some people do, ask for investors, and make small movies on someone else's dime. But, that's just not who I am as indie films rarely make their money back. But, to have a powerhouse company behind you, where money is no object, that is the pinnacle of the dream.

But, why does Netflix give that much money to filmmakers? Why does anyone give anyone money? Because there is a return. Whether that return is making money or getting something that they want from that someone they gave money to, there is always a deal in place—an expected return. In the case of Netflix, they have developed the vehicle to pay money to make money—all they need is someone to do it for them. But, when you have no way in, there is no way in. Then what?

So, here is the question(s) for the day… What do you want from someone? Why do they have a reason to give it to you? How will you/how can you pay them back? How can you make it worth their while?

Everyone wants something. Usually that wanting involves someone else giving you something. The thing is, most people are not worthy of receiving what they want, that's why they don't get it. So again, what do you want from something? How have you made yourself worthy of receiving it?

* * *
19/Oct/2020 07:15 AM

The person with the advantage is always the one who wants to challenge you to a fight.

* * *
18/Oct/2020 07:48 AM

If you are saying anything but good things you are saying the wrong things.

* * *
18/Oct/2020 07:48 AM

Sometimes you've got to clean house.

*   *   *

17/Oct/2020 01:12 PM

Most people spend their entire life trying to become something that they are not.

*　　*　　*

16/Oct/2020 03:33 PM

You can't answer a question that hasn't been asked.

* * *
14/Oct/2020 08:22 AM

You can't win an argument with a liar because all they will do is tell another lie.

* * *
13/Oct/2020 01:03 PM

It seems that people always have an excuse or a justification for their bad behavior.

What is yours?

*   *   *

13/Oct/2020 09:26 AM

What would you undo or redo if you could?

Why can't you?

The Anatomy of a Lie
13/Oct/2020 07:02 AM

  I think 2020 has been a strange year for all of us due to the COVID-19 coronavirus pandemic and all that. In some ways, early on, it almost seemed like it was going help the planet in some abstract way. I mean, the air got so much clearer because no one was driving, wild animals were roaming the streets in some locations, airplanes weren't in the sky, people got to spend more time with their family, and there seemed to be a calm returning to the world. That was all pretty short lived, however.

  There have been worse pandemics. Proportionality, more people died from the 1918 Flu. And, lost in the realms of history entire populations have been wiped out from causes known and unknown. Death and lost is never a good thing. But, that's the reality of all our lives.

  For me, my life never changed that much as I kind of exist out here on the extremities anyway. But, like most, I was kept from doing a lot of things I hoped to do. But again, that's the reality of all of our lives, sometimes thing are out of our control.

  Before I get too far off target here, let me begin… This will all tie together in a moment…

  About a week ago, someone backed into one of our cars at the supermarket, didn't leave any info, and just took off. That's not the first time something like that has happened to me but whenever something like that happens it does raise the flags of annoyance because you gotta deal with the repercussions. …They left a pretty big dent in the rear bumper. So, we called up the insurance company and they told us the place to take the car and it was all setup to be fixed. No big deal.

Picked it up yesterday and it wasn't a perfect job but what are you going to do? As someone who has been refinishing guitars for decades, I understand paint and I know you can get a perfect match to a color if you try. But, most everyone is so lackadaisical in their approach to their job and their life they just never seek any level of perfection. They didn't even wash or polish the car like most body shops do when they compete a job. I left, my lady remain to finish things up.

The thing that occurred, and what all of this blibber-blabber is actually about is, what the girl who set up the repair did next. I was gone due to not being happy with the job and I didn't want to raise a fuss. As my lady was finishing up the paperwork the employee of the body shop went into a complete lie about what had occurred when I dropped off the car. She told my lady that she had dawn up the paper work, I had checked it out, and had approved everything. That is not true. What actually happened is that she said it would take twenty minutes or so to do the paper work and if I wanted to wait I could. I said, no thanks, just email it to us. I got an Uber and went home. Moreover, she went into a whole lie about some sap that was now on the car. Where that came from, I don't know? But, they didn't even clean it off or rub it out. And, as you may or may not know, sap can really damage paint. Again, she lied and told my lady that we had discussed all that. We did not.

Why do people lie? Why do people lie so easily? Obviously, this young lady was very well practiced in the art of lying as she so easily went down that road. And, that's the thing about lying and liars, it is an acquired skill.

I have known a few liars in my life. People who lie and it is seemingly for no reason. But, why do they lie? What is their internal motivation for the lie? In the case of this young lady, I am sure it was some weird defense mechanism in order to keep her job in good standing or to make the work she did look better than it actually was. But, does that change the lie? No it does not. A lie is a lie is a lie and it will never be the truth. But, once a lie is told, it can never be retracted. This is especially the case with a person you will never see again. And, just maybe, that is why some people lie, they think they will never see that other person again. But again, that does not change the lie. And, a lie has the potential to set a whole destiny of further actions, reactions, and choices into motion.

Have you ever had a person lie to you and then go into a whole further defense for their lie once the lie was revealed? Have they additionally tried to orchestrate another lie to cover up the original lie with further lies? I know I have experienced that. It's weird; right? You know they lied. They know they lied. Yet, they re-lie to reposition the original lie. But, it is all still a lie. And, a lie that leads to another lie never changes the original lie.

So, here we are in life; 2020. The pandemic is still ranging, though society has somewhat opened up. Is it any better? No, not really. Did anybody learn anything and/or become a better human being? No, doesn't look like it. People are still doing the same things. Bumping into cars, taking off, and taking no responsibility for their actions. They are still lying to cover up their shoddy work or for who knows what reason???

Life is the same. People are the same. It is only you who can choose to make yourself a better vehicle of existence. Vehicle; get it?

Me, what could I do? I just wrote a one star review of the body shop on Yelp.

Marketing Consciousness
12/Oct/2020 08:50 AM

Most people don't think about rising consciousness. Most people don't think about enlightenment. Most people do not try to view the psychological problems they have and attempt to fix them. Most people don't think about making themselves a better vehicle of humanity. Most people just think about what they want which causes them to act in a less than ideal manner throughout their entire life.

Of the people that do think about higher consciousness, there is a small subset of those people who seek to become a teacher of consciousness. They seek to be the catalysis of helping others to become the best person that they can be. But, why does a person desire to become a teacher? What makes them believe that they have that key? Is it a true calling? Or, is it simply ego?

When we look to some of the individuals who have taken to the pulpit in modern years, we see that people like Tony Robbins, Deepak Chopra, Wayne Dyer, and Warner Erhart. These are a few of the key figures that have been at the forefront of the non-religious rising human consciousness marketplace. They have all sold a lot of books, tapes, CDs, DVDs, and seminars. People paid for them to live the lifestyle that they lived.

For each of these people, they became noted in their field, and for better or for worse they became the teacher to many of those few people who do seek to take their consciousness to a more refined level of existence. But why? Was it their vast unknowable knowledge, that only they possessed, or was it simply their ability to find a grand marketing plan?

For someone who came to any of these teachers and came away feeling that they were a better, more actualized individual because of what they learned, they left with a good experience. For others, who did not find what they had paid for, they walked away unhappy with the experience and blamed their teacher. But, who was right and who was wrong? The teacher for teaching or the student for not learning?

In all teaching situations, the student is the one who does or does not learn. In all learning environments, it is the student who is to blame for their not learning. From this, comes all kinds of culpability, however. As a dissatisfied student always blames the teacher. But, at the very root of human consciousness is the understanding that it is the person (themselves) who must learn and who must change if they hope to gain from any learning experience they entered into.

What does this tell us? First of all, the question must be asked, why is the teacher teaching? The answer is, the very elemental understanding of being a teacher is that someone believes that they know something that their underlings do not. Thus, what any/all teachers base their entire existence upon is ego. They are the teacher, you are the learner. They know something that you do not and their ego propels them to teach it to you. In some cases, these teachers find a great marketing plan and they are allowed to spread their knowledge to millions. But, does that guarantee that they are a good, true, and enlightened individual? No, not at all. That just means they have a good public relations team.

Many times, a student will initially appreciate what they are learning from a teacher and even like their teacher. But, human nature is a fickled thing. People change their mind. Maybe the teacher says something or does something they don't like or someone else places an idea in their head and all their good feelings about a teacher or a teaching changes. We have seen this in small or large examples with all of the teachers previously mentioned. But, what changed? Who changed? The teacher? The teaching? Or, the student?

All this leads us to the necessary analysis of who is seeking what and why? Why does the student seek to raise their consciousness or refine their psychology? And, do they possess the mental ability to do so?

For anyone who has taught anyone anything, it becomes quickly apparent that there are some good learners and then there are some angry students who seek to challenge the teacher. The motivation for this can come from any number of sources but the outcome is always the same, disruption in the teaching.

For the students that are seeking a higher knowledge and better self-awareness they are most probably the easiest to convince. The reason for this is that they want to learn, they hope to become better. This being the case, this is also the reason they are the most gullible as they are the easiest to shape into a believer. But, what is the price of belief? Isn't this where one has the penitential of being taken advantage of?

So, with all this being said, if you want to learn, if you care enough about the greater enlightenment of humanity, if you care about making yourself a better more highly functional person, where can you go to learn? I don't know. The teachers are all so filled with their own ego, seeking their own self-gains that I have not met one of them that was a truly enlightened individual and was not seeking to line their own pockets and/or stoke their own ego by becoming that teacher. I wish I had something better to offer you. But, as long as there is a personality on the pulpit, someone claiming that they are teaching you something, than all you are witnessing is ego and not true knowledge even though some are touted as being true knowers.

Look to the teacher who is teaching you. If you like what they have to say, learn from it. But, if they are charging you for their knowledge, they are not a true teacher. Because enlightened knowledge is always given for free.

***

12/Oct/2020 08:49 AM

If everyone believes something to be true that is not actually true does that make it true even though it is false?

Desired Destiny Unlived
11/Oct/2020 09:06 AM

Once upon a time, in the long ago and the far far away, I meet this very cute waitress at this restaurant I used to frequent all the time. Had situations been different, I believe there is a good chance that we probably would have hooked up. In any case, she had moved down to L.A. with her new husband in order that he could become the filmmaker he desired to be. Each time I would see her she would complain that he was sitting at home and doing nothing—not doing anything to pursue his dream. At one point she asked me to have a talk with him, which I did. But, I get it... Nobody wants to hear some other dude telling him what he should or could be doing. Thus, they moved back to Sacramento where she told me she was going to leave him as soon as he was resettled near his family because the guy was just not the man who she thought he would be or who he promised he would become.

Once upon a time, in the long ago and the far far away, I was teaching a class on filmmaking at U.C.L.A. One of my students was this cute young woman who turned out to be the cousin of a filmmaker I knew who had turned out a couple of successful projects on his daddy's dime. We became friends and one day she showed up to class with this new Sony camera. It was actually the top of the line prosumer camera at the time. She wanted to be a cinematographer. I was about to go up on a new film so I asked her if she wanted to shoot it for me. I thought this would give her a great opportunity to get her hands dirty and see what indie filmmaking was all about. The night before the shoot she called me and asked if we could meet. Sure! I thought she wanted to go over some of the shots, the lighting, or something like that. We met at a Starbucks. She pulls out her camera and asks, *"How do I focus it?"* OMG! She had purchased this top of the line camera, had never used it, and didn't even know how to focus it. I had to cancel that weekend's shoot.

Desire is an interesting thing. We all have desires. There is something that we all want to be. There are things that we all want to do. The problem is, a desire does not guarantee that a person has the potential or the personal motivation to actually get that desire actualized. They may not have what it takes to, *"Get 'er done…"* Sure, sure, there are tons of people out there who have a desire and strive to actualize it. Though they try and try what they do turns into nothing. But, they can take pride in that. They tried! Others are not like, however. They have a desire. Maybe they even have the money behind them to make that desire a reality but they never have the internal motivation or dedication to bring that desire into reality.

How about you? Where do you exist in the spectrum of your desires? Do you try to make them a reality on a daily basis? Do you really try? Or, do you just move to L.A. with the hopes that your dreams will somehow find you? Do you just buy the best camera on the market and never learn how to focus it?

I lost track of those two people. Sad, because I liked both of them. The waitress girl moved her husband back to Sacramento. What happened to her next I do not know? My student, I gave her an A but then I give all my students an A. That's just the kind of instructor I am. After the class I never heard from her again. I wonder if she ever learned how to focus her camera?

* * *
11/Oct/2020 08:26 AM

What happens when you realize that what you thought that you knew was wrong?

What happens when you find out that what you believed is wrong?

Do you believe what other people believe is wrong? This means there are people who believe what you believe is wrong.

Who is right?

And, what do you do with the knowledge that what you believe is wrong?

Seeking Deeper Wisdom
10/Oct/2020 07:45 AM

One of the most common words used in Sanskrit to describe the concept of wisdom is, *"Viveka."* And, one of the most pressing facts about wisdom is that so few people ever pursue it. This is why it is such a respected element of a person's life and why it has come to define the life of so few. Ask yourself, *"How much time do I spend each day seeking deeper wisdom?"* The answer for most is, none.

Why is it that wisdom is such a respected commodity yet it is so rarely sought after? For most, I believe, this is due to the fact that there is no immediate pay off to finding or gaining wisdom. It is most probably not going to pay your rent and it doesn't feel all that great. I mean, there is no big adrenaline rush associated with it. Thus, for most, it is put on the backburner of their life if it is ever contemplated at all.

The other problem with wisdom, and its acquisition, is that there is no clear pathway to its attainment. It is not like a university degree where you go to school for so long, take a certain amount of classes, and if you pass them, you get a diploma. Wisdom is much more abstract than all that.

Think about the people you have considered to have possessed wisdom. Why do you feel they were wise? What did they think? What did they do? And, why and how did they arrive at that position of being wise?

This is one of the first things that one must ponder if they ever hope to walk the pathway towards viveka. They must define and understand what wisdom actually is.

The thing about wisdom is, in association with no clear pathway to its achievement, there is also no great reward for its being had. Sure, sure, there are a few teachers and humanitarians who have become greatly respected for being considered to be in possession of wisdom but, in many cases, this being revered did little to make their life any better except in the cases of those who rose to great standing in some religious community where they were adorned with money and gratitude but is that wisdom at all? Or, is that someone simply riding on the wave of ego?

So, here's the question, what does wisdom mean to you? Does it mean anything to you? Do you care about those who are wise? Do you spend anytime attempting to elevate your mind and your life understanding to a position of deeper wisdom? If you do, what techniques are you using? If you don't, why not?

Yes, wisdom can just happened via life experience. But, more common than not, it does not occur unless someone sets about on a path where wisdom can truly be encountered. Though there are any number of pathways of gaining wisdom, it can never be truly held unless one is consciously walking upon that pathway and deliberately attempting to encounter a space of deeper knowledge.

The thing about life—the thing about the life of most people is they seek everything but wisdom; they desire everything but wisdom because wisdom has no big pay off. ...At least not in terms of Life Stuff. But, a person who develops wisdom, though possible never being truly appreciated, is the one who understands. And, isn't understanding the greatest good, the great goal of life?

If you seek wisdom, you may not get paid for it. But, if you hold wisdom, your understanding of life and reality should be payment enough.

Take a moment; define wisdom in your own mind. Define what it means to you. Delineate those you believe hold wisdom. Think about, can you be wise. If so, how are you going to walk towards one of life's ultimate goals?

*   *   *

10/Oct/2020 07:12 AM

How much time do you spend lost in fantasy thinking about things that are never going to happen?

Finances and Ways to Never Get Paid
09/Oct/2020 09:46 AM

Every now and then I will come upon one of my books that has been translated and published in some new language. Sometimes someone from some country will hit me up and thank me for having my book translated into their native language. The only problem is, I had no idea that the book had been translated. The original publisher of the book never told me or paid me for the new edition, even though that is part of our deal.

For those books, translated into various languages, the publishers in those countries are supposed to pay me royalties. With very few expectations, of all the books of mine that have been translated into all kinds of languages, I have not been paid anything. Zero… I guess they just think, out of sight, out of mind. Not cool, but that's the way it is. What can I do about it?

The thing is… And, my problem with this whole equation, they are making money off of my writings. But me, the author, is not. That's just not right.

Sometime people offer my movies via offshore download sites. Movies they have no right to distribute. I've always been a big opponent of that. But, there is only so much anyone can do. So, they make money from them but me, the creator, I do not. Again, that is just not right.

The people that review my films on YouTube are making money off of them, because they have ads and stuff in association with their reviews. I never really thought that was fair. Do you? They had nothing to do with making the film but simply by talking about it and using copyrighted footage they make a living. I always found that to be a strange approach to life. Again, equally no money to the creator. I consider that theft. How about you?

Most of my new Zen Films and those older rediscover pieces I offer on YouTube for free. Really for free… With no ads or anything like that. (I hate ads on YouTube). So, I'm not making any money on those films. But, that's my choice. That's my gift to anyone who desires to watch. So, no money coming in from them but, that's okay. I'm just putting them out there as cinematic art. Make of it what you will.

The other day I was looking at some of my on-line music sales. I noticed that an obscure song I did in like 2001, for whatever reason, has been getting a number of downloads and plays. Me, I'm going to get like $55.00. At one cent per play that works out to like five-thousand downloads.

You know, ever since all of these music streaming services have taken over the music distribution industry, the artist gets paid like a penny per play, which I don't really think is fair or cool but at least we get paid. So, there is at least some level of honesty in all that.

In contrast, a couple of years ago this music licensing firm sold some of my EDM Techno music to this company to soundtrack their video game. I still haven't seen a dime from that deal.

We all need money to survive. I do. You do. You have your way of making yours. And, I have my way of making mine. But, the problem that comes into play is when other people climb into your sandbox. They want to play with your toys. But, they didn't bring any of their own toys along. They want what they want for free. They want to make money off of what someone else has created and they do not want to pay for the service. Is that right?

If you are a creator, I am sure you have pondered this question. If you are a consumer, maybe not. One way or the other, I believe it is important to actually think about what you are receiving; who is involved and how the people who are selling it to you came to the position of offering it to you in the first place. Mostly, what I am saying is I think you really need to look to the deeper aspects of consumption verses distribution and how what you consume actually affects the sourcepoint creation or the creator.

Think before you consume. Think about who is getting paid, who is not, and why.

*　　*　　*
08/Oct/2020 08:58 AM

Think about if all of the things you've killed or were involved with killing: ants, spiders, mosquitos, fish, cows came back to attack you.

Does any life want to be killed?

Montage and Who Cares About Anybody Anyway?
07/Oct/2020 03:07 PM

Have you ever had one of those days where your life kinda feels like a montage or a music video or something? …Kinda when events are so cinematic it is not like real life. That's kind of what went on with me today.

You know, like that great song, *"Montage,"* from the movie, *Team America World Police*.

Anyway, a friend of mine asked me to come by and lays down some notes on his new recording. I felt kind of weird because Eddie Van Halen just passed away yesterday. He was certainly one of the greatest rock players of all time. As far as I am concerned, to date, there has only been two people who truly changed rock n' roll guitar forever. The first was Jimi Hendrix and the second was Eddie Van Halen. Arguably, there were other players of his generation who may be considered better guitarist: Al Di Meola, Paco de Lucia, Jon McLaughlin, but his contribution to the evolution of rock n' roll guitar is undeniable.

I've noticed that MTV Classic is playing back-to-back Van Halen videos today. That's great! It was fun to sit back and watch a few of them and remember…

Anyway… I was a bit reluctant due to COVID-19 and all that but I thought everyone would be cool at the studio and they would do the social distancing thing and have all that worked out. So, I got in my car and clicked on one of my all time favorite band, Dinosaur Jr. and I let the music play. But, from the moment I got in the car everything changed.

I don't know what it is but is seems that everyone has forgotten how to drive. I first noticed this after the first lock down of COVID-19, when for a long while there was nobody on the road; even here in a place like L.A., then things started to open up and when people began to drive again they either forgot how to drive or they no longer cared about the fact that there are other people on the road. In about two or three miles three people had pulled out of streets or driveways, directly in front of me, and completely cut me off. Like one of those 3-D effects in a movie. Right there in your face.

I get to the studio. Walk in. And, it was like I had stepped back to 1980 something. I was wearing a mask but everyone else was just there hanging out like nothing was going on out in the world. Hell, the president just got COVID last week.

Everybody was sitting in this small room behind the board, talking and joking. They had coke laid out and people were snorting it.

Truthfully, I wish I could step back in time a few decades and powder my nose. But, it would probably kill me if I did it now. So, I passed on the offers. But, the scene it all looked like a music video. A bunch of rockers in a studio drinking, snoring coke, and recording music. So, strange…

Me, I just had to leave. I don't want to take the chance of getting sick.

I told my friend to send me what he had recorded and I would add something to it for him from my home studio if he still wanted me to. I mean, I get it… The whole thing of collaborating is interacting face-to-face. But, right now, this is just not the time to live what was going on at that studio.

Kind of like that great song and music video from Twenty-One Pilots, Level of Concern where the two guys are working in two different studios and then mailing what they have created to the other one only to find out, at the end of the video, that they live next door to each other. *"Would you be my little quarantine..."*

Anyway, I left. Listening to Dinosaur Jr. again; two more cars cut me off en route home.

I stopped as I needed gas and I watched as the people in this station were insanely selfish. I mean, don't you hate it when there are two pumps in a row and the person who got there first parks in the middle and takes up both spots. That, plus people snaking spots from one another and one guy backing up without looking and almost hitting the car that was trying to pull up to a spot but they saw him coming, slammed their car into reverse, and got out of the way. The guy obliviously drove on and didn't even notice what he had almost done.

It was weird... There was so much movement. It was like a Mechanical Ballet.

That's the other thing I've noticed since we've all gone outside again. Most people just don't seem to give a fuck. All they think about is themselves. But, I'll get to that in a minute.

The high point of my gas getting experience was that this attractive young woman pulls up and gets out of her car to pump her gas. She was total 1980s Video Vixen material. The way she flicked her hair back was so funny. If she had been in slow motion with a fan blowing her hair it could all have been a video production. Combine this with the fact that she was wearing a brand spanking new Iron Maiden tee shirt. It made me smile. How bizarre.

After getting my gas, I hopped back in my car, clicked back on and blasted Dinosaur Jr. as I drove home.

So... Here's the question(s) for the day... Take a moment an really think about each one...

What are the things that you care about?

What are the things that you think about in regard to the things that you care about?

What are the things you care about in regard to other people?

Do you change what you are doing to make someone else's something better or do you not think about anyone else but yourself at all?

Life is an interactive experience. You can either interact in a conscious manner or you just steam roll your way through your existence thinking about and caring only about yourself.

Who are you?

What do you do?

Do you ever think about any of this or anyone else?

Do you care about the people you don't know?

Do you jam out onto the street before you look to see if any other car is coming?

Do you take two spots at the pump at the gas station?

Do you back up without looking?

Or, do you wear a fun tee shirt that makes people smile?

Your life. Your choice. You can either make the world better or worse.

You Can Make Things Better
06/Oct/2020 07:20 AM

You can make things better.

If you've hurt someone, do something good for them, say something nice about them.

If you are feeling overwhelmed step outside, intentionally step away from the chaos. Turn off your mind. Take a walk.

If you are focusing on the negative and/or hating your life. Stop it! Turn it around. See the positivity in the negativity. Appreciate what you have.

If you are lonely, go outside; internationally introduce yourself to someone.

If you are unhappy; you can trace that unhappiness to its root and eliminate it if you have the time. If not, just stop it! You have the power. Go and do something you like. Go exercise. Replace the unhappiness with positive activity and the unhappiness will fade.

Just as negativity begins with you, so does positivity. You can choose to make things better.

Your yesterday does not have to be your today.

Be nice to people. Reach out to people. Do good things for people. Say good things about people. Do good things for yourself. Do this, and everything will become better.

* * *
06/Oct/2020 07:20 AM

No matter how hard you cry it will not change what has happened.

Power
05/Oct/2020 08:02 AM

I've recently been watching the HBO documentary series, *The Vow*. It's one of those weekly installment things that I always find a bit annoying as you have to wait until next week to see the next episode. For the people who watch it at a later date I guess this won't be a problem as once it is On Demand I am sure you will be able to binge it if you want. The doc is a bit filler-heavy and it would have been nice to cut it down to like an hour and a half. But, I get it, some filmmakers want to provide as much inside info as possible.

This doc is about NXIVM and it leader Keith Raniere and all its players and how they got to where they got be. First of all, I have no personal experience with NXIVM and I do not believe that I've ever personally known anyone who did. But, that is not what this piece is about. This piece is about power—the way some people attempt to unleash it, hold onto it, and how some people fall prey to it.

From my early years forward, I was drawn to spiritual teachings and making one's self and life better. So, throughout the years, I have interacted with a lot of spiritual teachers. I was a close member of Swami Satchidananda's Integral Yoga Institute and the Sufi Order in my teenage years. About this time, the whole Jim Jones, Jonestown thing took place and people started talking a lot about cults. As I have said before, in all of my years with Swami Satchidananda the only money I gave the group was a $10.00 donation when we were buying Gurudev a new blanket for the Los Angeles Integral Yoga Institute. In terms of time, I was happy to give it. These people were my friends and we were doing things together—doing things for the greater good. This is the same with martial arts, in all the years I professionally taught martial arts at a studio I never took one dime for myself. It was my donation to the greater good. The point? Spiritually does not have to be about a cult, power, getting people's money, and hurting people lives.

You can watch the HBO doc or read about the goings on of NXIVM if you want to know the kind of things Raniere and his people did to other people. But, that kind of behavior has nothing to do with spirituality! In fact, if anyone initially knew this kind of stuff was going on, they probably never would have walked through the door. And, that's the problem, people either do not know or they are forced into situations of surrendering their personal power and from there people have the ability to gain more power over others and tell them they must relinquishing their personal wholeness for some spiritual something. But, it's all a con. Spirituality and psychological betterment is never about giving some unenlightened individual the keys to your mind, your wholeness, and/or your wellness: spiritual, psychological, financial or otherwise.

In this doc, you see the kind of things the powers-that-be did to hurt the lives of those who left the group. You also see how parents think they know better than their children and they attempt to put the power play on them. But, no one is absolutely right and/or holy. Some people just think they are.

In life, I have witnessed this kind of power-based behavior a lot. For me, it never happened in spiritual groups. When I was ready to leave, I left. Everyone wished me all the best. In business, however—in the martial arts, in the film game, people truly hurt my life all as a means to attempt to show that they possessed power over me. Hell, even trolls on the internet, even reviewers, hoped to express their power over me by falsely judging me and bagging my creations.

In terms of parents, my father died when I was young but my mother totally fucked with my life attempting to hold onto power over me. For others, I have watched as their parents attempted to keep them from becoming all they could and all they wanted to be with whom they wanted to be with. In regard to Swami Satchidananda, many years back this one female devotee apparently met one of Satchidananda's swamis, they feel in love, he left the order, they got married, but her parents actually put up a website blaming their love on the Cult of Satchidananda. How is that finding of love his fault? How is finding love a bad thing?

As far as this doc goes, it shows the case of this one time kinda famous actress doing all she can to get her daughter out from under the influence of Raniere. She eventually provided the New York Attorney General with all kinds of evidence, including against her daughter. She says, *"If she has to go to jail, I guess that's better than her being with him."* What kind of mother says that? What kind of mother does something like that? What kind of mother puts her daughter in harm's way like that? What kind of power trip is that? Whatever the outcome, who is she to think for her daughter?

To understand some of the subtleties of what I am taking about you may have to view the doc. But, I think we can all understand power. The way some people try to exhibit it over others to control them, what people do to maintain it, and the damage it can cause to the lives of people who are forced to deal with the power plays of others. How about you? Have you been dominated by the power of someone else? How about you? Have you attempted to dominate someone else with your power? Why? Why to them and why to you?

If we look at the exhibition of power, it comes from a very low level of human consciousness. It arises from a position of insecurity. Why does anyone want to have power over someone else? Answer, because they are not whole in themselves and they need to feel the drug that they are something more than that someone else.

I am sure Raniere and his cronies (and/or anyone else from any other group or just a solo person) were/are in denial about why they were doing what they were doing; just as most people who seek power over others are. They can make up excuses, they can tell themselves (and others) lies, they can gain a feeling of empowerment, raised adrenaline, and even false holiness by exhibiting power over others. But, all that is a lie. It is one of the ultimate deceptions of life. Sure, maybe you win the fight but if you hurt someone's life evolution in the process what are the consequences to you, your destiny, and to all of those you lured into playing in your game? In the case of Raniere, potentially the rest of his life in prison. For his disciples, long prison sentences. Power is a bad thing. Think before you seek it.

* * *

05/Oct/2020 07:13 AM

Are all conversations worth having?

* * *
05/Oct/2020 07:13 AM

Are all memories worth remembering?

Reading Your Own Meaning into the Message
04/Oct/2020 07:25 AM

This is a subject that I've touched on in the past but every now and then I am contacted by someone (in some fashion) and they are translating something that I wrote completely by their own definition. The only problem is, they are reading something into what I wrote that I did not intend.

When one of these situations occurs it always send to smilingly remember this one time a friend of mine and I were having lunch and he pulls out a small a notebook where he had taken notes about what I had said a few days before and he wanted me to explain and translate what I was actually thinking and what I actually meant. *"It meant nothing,"* I exclaimed.

I am not one of those people who composes hidden meanings into what I write. I find that kind of stuff way too pretentious and frankly just bullshit. I write what I write. I try to explain what I am thinking in the best way that I can and then I move on. Sometimes, I rethink a subject and realize I did not explain my thought process in a complete fashion so I readdress the issue. But, that's about as deep as it gets. I am not sending you any hidden messages.

This is the same with life. I'm a very honest person. I do not hide or pretend or play head games. I'm just me.

This subject is something I think that everyone needs to examine in their own life and analyze how it causes them to interpret what other people say and do and how it causes them act and react.

Are you looking for a deeper meaning in what someone has to say? Are you seeking hidden messages? The thing is, if a person operates their life by believing that they have some hidden truth that no one else knows they are either lying to other people or they are lying to themselves. There are no secrets!

If someone thinks that they hold the position in life that they are so all-powerful that they need to relay things to the initiated in a secret manner they are operating from a position of vanity and ego. Does a person who holds the mindset that they are so much of something that they must pass on hidden directives truly deserve your loyalty and your servitude?

So, where does this lead us? It leaves us with life. Some people just look to seek out the hidden meaning. Some people want to be part of that inner group who believes that they know something and they are in communication with someone on some secret level that no one else can understand. If that's what you want to do, that's great, that's life; good luck. You're just not going to find it here. ☺

       *   *   *
03/Oct/2020 06:48 PM

It is easy to say you don't like somebody.

It is easy to criticize somebody.

It is easy to make snide comments about somebody.

What is much harder is to put yourself on the frontlines and actual do something that makes this world a better place.

Actions Have Consequences
03/Oct/2020 08:14 AM

I was happily asleep this morning; lost deeply in realms of a vivid dream when someone's nearby car alarm went off and woke me up. How annoying! I don't know why people still have car alarms as no one breaks into cars anymore. But, it woke me up. Don't you hate car alarms? The problem is, I am one of those people that once I am awoken I can't easily go back to sleep. So, I was forced to get up way before I wanted to. Someone did something; they set off their car alarm and it affected the life of someone else in a non-positive manner. Is that right? Is that the way life should be?

I was at the supermarket yesterday. I had purchased my groceries, loaded them in my car, and was heading for the parking lot exit. A young African-American man bolts in front of me in a new sedan, cutting me off. No big deal, whatever… Just as he was about to pull out from the parking lot he throws his fast food drink out of his window onto the asphalt. The cup, the ice, the straw, and the remaining drink splatter everywhere. I had not seen anything like that in years. Who does that kind of stuff? How rude! I honk my horn at him. …Like what the fuck? He drives on. Again, here is someone who unconsciously, uncaringly did something that affected the life of someone (many people, in fact) in a non-positive manner. Is that right? Is that the way life should be?

A couple of months ago, just after all of the #icantbreathe and #blm riots broke out I was taking an afternoon walk. I have always enjoyed walking around my neighborhood (wherever I am living) or wherever I find myself in the world. It is a great way to see and touch life and they say it is good for your health. I live in what may be considered an affluence neighborhood. Certainly, my dwelling is not. But, the neighbor is... Anyway, I was walking to one of my local parks with my lady when this young African-American family gets out of their semi rundown car in the park's parking lot. I didn't think much about it. I just assumed they were probably not from the neighborhood. As we approached each other, walking in opposite directions, the male of the crew bumps into me, obviously attempting to instigate a confrontation. Me, I smiled at him. How can you fight a smile?

Ever since those young African-American men were asked to leave Starbuck in New York because they didn't buy a drink a couple of years ago and ended up getting paid millions due to their lawsuit, there has been a certain type of person who has sought ways to make money for nothing. Certainly, this is nothing new. People have instigated and/or faked car accidents and personal injuries in establishments in order to get paid forever. But, every now and then it seem due to the climate of the time people get motivated to find ways to get paid via devious means. So again, here is someone instigating a non-positive action that has the potential to have negative affects on the life of someone else. Is that right? Is that the way life should be?

Most people are not that contriving, however. Most people simply act, react, and do as they do as they pass through their life. Like the person who unconsciously set off their car alarm the morning, did their thoughts go to the lives of people who were sleeping and they woke up? Probably not. Did the young man who threw the drink out of his car window care about the maintenance people who were going to have clean up his mess or the people who were going to have look at the trash he threw on the ground? Probably not. He was just done with his drink and didn't want the cup in his new car.

Everything you do has the potential to affect someone else. The question then has to be asked, are you thinking about how your actions are affecting that someone else? Moreover, do you care? Or, are you only thinking about <u>your</u> moment or maybe even how you can get paid for doing nothing but creating havoc in someone else's life space?

Actions have consequences. What you do will come to affect you. How you live your life will come to define your life. The things you do—particularly the things you do that affect other people will set what you encounter next into motion. Maybe you won't meet your consequences today but they will find you.

How do you want to live your life? Are you going to <u>do</u> with a conscious respect and appreciation for others and all things life or are you just going to <u>do</u> whatever it is you want to do without a thought?

Your life. Your consequences.

*   *   *

02/Oct/2020 01:55 PM

How much time do you spend everyday trying to make things better?

...Not just for you but for everyone?

The Things That You Think and Is Reality What You Really Think It Is?
02/Oct/2020 07:08 AM

Life is a long process of living, exploring, learning, and disseminating. When people have time (and money) on their hands they seek out things that are not essential to everyday survival—they seek distraction. These distractions take on many-many forms. The one thing that is true to all distractions, however, is that they are not made up of the absolute essentials of life and survival.

When people have time on their hands they look to find something to desire, they look to find something to believe in, they look to find something to do. But, is doing with no greater purpose something worth doing at all or is it simply wasting time?

Once people find a focus of their distracted life they pursue that focus. Some focus on the realities of life. Others focus on far more abstract objects and ideologies. The question that must always be questions, however, is what is real in the what you are seeking? Is what you are watching, hearing, and/or desiring real or is it simply part of the grander illusion of life?

Think about all of the people who were once believed to be true and honest and then turned out to not be telling the truth. Have you been lied to? Have you lied to others? Simply by following that pathway of thought you can quickly realize that all someone says does not necessarily equal the truth. So, what do words actually mean if you cannot believe them?

People desire things in their pursuit of distraction. Think about how many people have gone into debt buying the things of their desire. Have you? Did your acquired desire equal what you thought it would in your life?

In the acquisition of desired object we have all heard about forgeries and fakes being sold as something that is real. But, is a forgery or a fake any less of an acquisitionable object if one believes that it is something that is true?

I think to my friend Kris Derrig. (God rest his soul). He was one of those very nice, very soft spoken people. For a vocation, he was a master of creating guitars. He was a true master luthier. His specialty was making what appeared to be vintage Gibson Les Paul guitars circa 1958 and 1959. (I have an article on this site about him). Were they true Gibson guitars? No. But, they were as good as the best of anything Gibson ever turned out. Sadly, Kris passed away many-many years ago at the age of thirty-two from lung cancer. Soon after that, due to the rise to fame of the band Guns and Roses and the fact that Slash and the other people like Lenny Kravitz used guitars that he made, his creations became highly sought after and now go for a very high price. Again, were they a true Gibson guitar? No. But, though they are a, *"Fake,"* does that make them any less of a playable instrument? No, it does not.

So, here is the question, what is true and what is real? Is truth only the perspective of the person who is telling the lie? And, is real only the question of how well something is constructed and how desirable of an acquisition it becomes?

* * *
02/Oct/2020 07:07 AM

Nothing ever changes if you don't choose to make a change.

*   *   *
01/Oct/2020 10:32 AM

What happens when you believe something about a person and it turns out to not be true?

* * *

30/Sep/2020 09:47 AM

Did you read the instructions?

* * *

30/Sep/2020 09:41 AM

It seems everybody wants to tell you how you should live your life.

It appears everybody wants to judge the decisions that you have made.

If a person is truly whole and self-actualized they say nothing because they understand everybody is perfect onto themselves.

Love
30/Sep/2020 07:06 AM

The Sanskrit word, *"Prem,"* is probably the most common word associated with the concept of love used in the Sanskrit language. Though there are a number of words that can be used to describe the various factors of love in Sanskrit, (as Sanskrit is a very advanced language), *"Prem,"* is the most commonly used and refers to a total or unconditional love.

How much time do you spend thinking about love? How much time do you spend giving love? How much time do you spend loving someone or something?

For most, the concept of love is very prevalent especially in the minds of the young. For many, they believe that love is the ultimate answer. They hold a belief that when they find love all will become right with the world. You can see this is the eyes of many a young woman. They see a man that they like, they meet a man that they like, they are invited out by a man that they like, and they hold the belief that all will work out as they have seen in their dreams. This is why so many young women are lead astray via the unscrupulous male.

Men are not that much different. They hold onto finding and being in love with that woman of their dreams. They go out in order to meet that woman. You can always see a man, particularly as they become older, who is searching for love. They go to restaurants and chat up the waitress believing that the smile they receive means something more than simply a person hoping to get a good tip. I have known men that have courted strippers, who were not interested in them at all, in the strangest ways; even going to the club where they worked, paying lots of money for lap dances and the like, hoping to see them outside of the workplace; which never happened. Of course, there are the stalkers, but they are a whole other breed in themselves. But again, just someone who is looking for love. Just in a very messed up way.

For people that have found what they believe is love, and follow the relationship road, many/most find that it is never quite what they anticipated and/or hoped for. This is what leads to so many breakups. But, for many, the moment they are out of one relationship they seek another. They again are looking for love.

But, what is love? Is love getting a person that you find desirable to be with you and only you? Is love getting everything you want from a person? Is love getting that need for love met by that one person? If so, why do so many stray from their relationship(s) of love?

I think to what my teacher, Swami Satchidananda, used to say about love. *"It's like doing business. I love you honey. Oh, I love you too honey. I don't love you anymore. Then I don't love you either."* In many ways this is true. Love is like doing business. But, is that the way love should be?

Many people make love a very thoughtless, physical thing. It is all about them getting what they want. They meet someone and that person touches that spot of love in them and so they love them until that spot is no longer touched. Again, is that true love?

People make love a drug. A drug that can only be had from that certain someone else. Maybe that drug will keep them high for a minute, maybe for years, but as it is a drug, that sensation will eventually fade. But, is that love?

From a spiritual understanding, love is much deeper that all of this. Love is something that emulates from inside of you. It is in you.

Try this… Take a moment right now. I am sure we have all felt love, so we all know what it feels like. Right now, close your eyes and find that place of love within you. Locate that Love Center in your being. Feel that feeling of love. Let it expand and encompass you.

Depending on your current state of mind, you can allow that feeling of love to truly overpower you or you can just acknowledge that, yes, there it is. Yes, it is inside of you.

By performing this exercise you quickly realize that you do not need someone else to make you feel that experience of love. You can feel love no matter who you are with even if you are all alone. By allowing yourself to acknowledge that you do not need someone else to experience love, you become free from the entire process of seeking out love.

Now, certainly love feels very good. Being in love with someone else makes you feel great. But, though someone else may stimulate that feeling of love within you, it is still you who is the one experiencing it.

For your next exercise try this… Next time you are with someone (someone that you do not and/or did not previously love) allow yourself to love him or her. Allow them to be the catalyst for you to feel love. In fact, walk down a crowded street and love everyone.

The thing is, love is already inside of you. You are the one who decides whether or not to love someone. You can be very specific in who you love or you can allow love to become you and from this you can love everyone.

People seek out that feeling of love. Many quest their entire life for it. But, as you are the one who does or does not feel love, that means you are the one who can control whether or not you feel love.

Try allowing love to just be a part of you. Try loving everyone you meet and/or interact with. Love, and everything becomes better. Love, and anger, deception, hurting, and wars will all end. Why? Because if you love everyone, why would you want to hurt anyone?

* * *
29/Sep/2020 05:25 PM

Ama todo lo que existe en este momento y serás libre.

Residuals
29/Sep/2020 01:56 PM

For those of you who may not know, Residuals are what an actor, a director, a screenwriter, or a composer gets paid every time a union film or TV production is shown. The film professionals get paid a standardized fee up front, then, when that production is rebroadcast, they get a certain percentage of that fee. Sometimes these checks only add up to a few pennies but it's the thought that counts.

Residuals were created in the 1960s by the then Screen Actors Guild to assure that the performers and the filmmakers were fairly compensated throughout the entire time a production is seen—wherever it is seen. From this, not only do the production companies and the producers make a fair wage but also so do all of the other people associated with the production.

Personally, I am an active member of the SAG/Aftra Union. Thus, I cannot act in non-union productions. Thank you to all of you indie producers out there for asking me to take part in your production but due to my union status I cannot.

The reason that the union is a great thing is that it makes sure everyone is paid fairly. Every time any segment of a union production is broadcast anywhere it is required that those people or that company broadcasting it pay for the usage of that production so that everyone is rightly compensated. Enter the internet and this has all changed.

Many people watch illegal downloads of films and TV shows all the time. Do they even care about what their watching that illegal download is doing to the financial stability of the cast and crewmembers? Probably not. Like the FBI states, *"Internet Piracy is not a Victimless Crime."*

On sites like YouTube some people upload films that they do not own the rights to—reviewers take segments of films, in large or small qualities, and pay nothing for the film's usage. Though they are making money via the number of viewers they have and the advertisements on YouTube, the actual film's creators are receiving no payment. Is that fair that someone who had nothing to do with the creation of the film is making money but the cast and crewmembers are not? This is why residual payments were instigated in the first place.

This is where one of the big problems with SAG/Aftra, the Producers Guild (PGA), the Directors Guild (DGA), and the American Society of Composers, Authors, and Publishers (ASCAP) arises. They do not police their own policies. In some cases, some of the large production companies will immediately go after anyone who broadcasts all or part of one of their productions. And, if you look at the online reviewers, most of them stay away from these films because they do not want to receive copyright takedown noticed because after they receive three (at least on YouTube) their account is nullified. And yes, even the small producers can go after the people who take footage from their films, but it can become a headache so many do not.

The fact is, somewhere/someone came up with the concept of Fair Use. Many reviewers believe that this gives them the right to take footage from anyone's film that they want. But, if you check the law, Fair Use was designed for learning institutions and established news agencies, not for someone to make money off of a film by putting up a review. And, like I have stated in many places, the moment you make one penny off of someone else's production, Fair Use goes out the window and copyright infringement comes into play. If you doubt this fact ask any attorney who specializes in copyright law.

The copyright law is the copyright law but what does any of that mean if no one is willing to follow it? Moreover, there is a world full of people happy to waste their time on sites like YouTube doing nothing but watching whatever nonsense is being broadcast.

In a perfect world, people would care about other people. And, this is the point of this piece. Caring... Caring enough to care. The question you always must ask yourself is how is what you are doing affecting the life of that someone else? How is what you are doing creating havoc in the life of someone you have focused your attention upon? For the reviewers, if you care enough to take the time to view a film and then review it, shouldn't you also care about the people who created that film? Isn't that only right? For the viewers, do you ever contemplate how what you are doing, as seemingly innocent as it may be, will affect the life of someone else? Or, do you just do what you do and never think about the bigger picture? If that is the case, I would really suggest that you take a long hard look at your life. Because right is always right and wrong is always wrong.

In closing, the rules, the residuals, and taking the time to care were all set up in order to make the all and the everything of life better. Are you making life better? If you are hurting anyone in the process of what you are doing, you are not making it better. Is that right?

Always Help. Always think. Always care. Think about the other person—think about how what you are doing will affect that other person. Think about someone else beside yourself. Do what you do with a conscious caring purpose and all of life becomes better. And, don't rob the livelihood of someone via your own selfish needs.

* * *

29/Sep/2020 07:45 AM

If a person lies to you once they are probably going to lie to you again because everything that they built your relationship upon is based upon a falsehood.

* * *
29/Sep/2020 07:34 AM

How many people believe in a religion that other people believe is false?

If a specific religion was the absolute truth wouldn't everyone believe in it?

We All Owe Somebody Something
28/Sep/2020 09:07 AM

We all owe somebody something. Throughout all of our lives there have been people who have taught us things, opened doors for us, and if it were not for them we would not be who and what we ultimately become.

In some cases, our memory of and our reverence for these people is very prominent in our minds. In other cases, we pretend that they do not exist and that they did not help us. In fact, in some cases, some people are so self-involved that they do not even realize the help someone gave them. In any of these cases, this does not change the fact that there have been people in all of our lives that have helped us.

I think to the many martial artists I have known over my fifty plus years of involvement in these systems of self-defense. Early on, I realized that many of the practitioners, who became teachers, began to extradite the people who taught them from their life. As they personally came to hold a more prominent position of influence they did not want their students to know where the basis of their knowledge came from. This was particularly the case if they had trained under the lineage of a Western instructor. This ideology may have been based in the fact that they did not want their students to go to the source where they gained their knowledge or it may have been simply based in ego. Whatever the case, many removed their true teachers from their résumé. In some cases, these practitioners would replace their true teachers with some mythical Asian instructor that was impossible to locate. In other cases, they would associate themselves with an Asian-based teacher or organization in order to appear to be closer to the true source of the system. In either/any case, who was truly owed what became hidden.

In the film industry, I have also witnessed people removing the people who have truly opened a door for them from their résumé. As I have long stated, the film industry is an impossible game. Though thousands/millions of people hope to become part of it every year, very few find their way in. And, virtually anyone who does accomplish this is guided in via someone opening the door for them. Yet, if an individual becomes successful, that door-opening, helpful person is very commonly overlooked. Again, this may be based in ego or it may be based in a person hoping to appear to be more than they actually are. Whatever the case, the true person who is owed something is ignored.

People help us on all levels of our life. Whether it was a specific teacher in school or someone at the workplace. Maybe it was simply someone who was a good friend when we needed one. Whatever the case, we all owe somebody something.

Take a look at the world around you. Take a look at the successful people that you know. How did they get there? Were they not helped by someone? In fact, take a look at the successful people that you know, do you ever question who helped them obtain their success and whom they are not thanking for the help they received?

Everyone who rises to any level of anything has been helped: the martial arts instructor, the movie star, the film director, the author, the musician, the teacher, the journalist, the broadcast journalist, the manager at the company, the book reviewer or the online movie reviewer who speaks about other peoples creations; they did not write the book, they did not make the film so they owe the creator who actually did, a lot. They have a job because of that author or because of that filmmaker. The list goes on and on and on. You simply have to open your eyes to see the truth about who is owed what and if other people, (and if you), are willing to give credit where credit is do.

So… Here's the exercise for the day… First of all look outwards to the people that you know and know of who have become successful. Who did they learn from? Who opened a door for them? Who helped them get to where they are? And, do they give credit where credit is due?

Once you have thoroughly explored that level of your life and your life relationships turn the microscope on you. And, it's important to be very honest with yourself… Think about your life… Think about where you find yourself in life… Who helped you get to where you are? Who passed on knowledge to you that helped you grow in life? Who opened a door for you? Who created something that allowed you to move forward towards becoming who you hoped to be?

Help arises from so many levels of life that they cannot all be listed. For each person it is different. Who do you owe what to and why? And, are you willing to give credit where credit is due?

We all owe somebody something. If you don't pay your debt all you become is an individual based in deception.

Give credit where credit is due. Thank those who have helped you in either a small or a large way. Believe me, it makes everything just a little bit better.

* * *

27/Sep/2020 07:32 AM

How many times has your guardian angel saved you from disaster and you didn't even know it?

The Birthday Buddha
25/Sep/2020 09:16 AM

It was my birthday the other day.

Birthdays always strike me as kinda strange. I mean everybody makes such a big deal about it being their birthday. And, I guess for some it does become a big deal. But, for me, it never was really like that. I was an inner-city only child, whose parents were way more focused on their careers than me, so I never had birthday parties or anything like that. The one time I did have a kinda cool birthday experience was when I was still a teenage. As I was already long involved with the Eastern Spiritual Tradition, I was on the staff of a spiritual retreat for the Integral Yoga Institute. Someone, somehow figured out it was by B'day and they spread it around. What occurred was that the head Swami decided we had to go out. So, we snuck away from all the, *"Retreaters,"* who were all in their cabins meditating or asleep and they took me to a local restaurant up in the Santa Monica Mountains, where the retreat we being held, where we had carrot cake. That was pretty cool.

Mostly, on my B'days, wherever I am in the world, here in L.A., or elsewhere, I try to do, at least one small thing, spiritually focused. Normally, I go to a temple or something like that.

Last year I was in Singapore on my B'day so I went to this Hanuman temple I like there. This year, as I was in L.A., I normally have a few choices as there are some very nice Buddhist and Hindu temples in the greater L.A. area. The problem is/was, COVID-19. They are all closed. Not open. So, I could not go to one.

Sure, sure, I get it, the true temple is inside all of us. But, I still like to take in the energy of an intentional spiritual setting. But, not this year. Thanks China!

Most people hope to receive gifts on their B'day. I have this one extended family member who used to fax (remember those) out her wish list every birthday. I always thought that was kinda funny. Me, long ago, I decide it was a way more cool thing to give someone else a gift on my birthday. And, I have always continued to do that.

One B'day, way back in the way back when, I gave my then girlfriend a Rolex. The relationship eventually went South. So, I don't know if going that elaborate is a great thing to do. But, giving always seems to be the best thing to do (on any occasion) but birthdays seem like the ideal time.

So... Just the suggestion for the day, the year, whatever... Your next B'day, don't only think about yourself and what you want. Think about someone else and maybe give them what they want.

Giving always seems to be the best medicine.

*　　*　　*
25/Sep/2020 08:49 AM

When somebody gives you advice and it turns out to be the wrong advice is their fault for giving it to you or your fault for taking it?

All the Things That You Think You Know
24/Sep/2020 09:38 AM

What do you know? What do you think you know? Why do you think you know it?

I imagine we have all been in one of those situations where we were somewhere and someone is talking about something and we believe we know something about the subject of which they speak. Of course, people talk about so much stuff, it is almost unfathomable. So, whatever someone has the potential of talking about runs the gambit of all reality. But, every now and then, I am sure, someone is saying something, and you feel like you really need to chime in and add your thoughts to the conversation. Do you? This is one of the questions that defines who you are as a human being. Are you one of the outspoken KNOWERS? Or, are you simply a person who believes you know what you believe you know and keeps it to yourself?

In all conversations, people speak about what they think about—they talk about what they believe they know. That's just life. But, how often is what they say (is what you say) based simply upon something you heard which then lead you to your beliefs? How often is what you say simply based in some self-concocted ideology based on nothing more than some opinion that emulated from your own mind? Moreover, how often is what you say wrong?

There is this great trick of manipulation that has been going on on-line forever. The trick is, someone posts a comment stated as a fact and attaches maybe a photo or a video about some-something. Then, that same person, via a different account, or perhaps one of their cohorts quotes that statement and references that photo or video in order to make what they are saying sound like it is based in fact. But, is it? This technique can go on and on from there. It has the potential to expand exponentially. But, is belief—is desired opinion a fact or is it simply what a person believes based in whatever concoction of principles and philosophies that person holds? And, does believing a lie propagated by another person ever become the truth no matter how often it is quoted or referenced?

It really comes down to the question, how much of anyone's life (how much of your life) is based upon actual fact compared to how much of life is based upon belief, opinion, and/or a desired ideology that someone wants others to hold? Do you ever think about this as you are obtaining knowledge? Do you ever think about this before you believe your beliefs? Do you ever think about this before you chime into a conversation and put in your two-cents?

Life is based in a person's belief that spreads outwards to others. Beliefs may be believed by a small or a large number of people. But, does a belief actually mean anything? Does anyone speaking what they think they know mean anything if what they are saying is based upon nothing more than what they think concocted from a credo spread forward from the mind of someone who has no basis in truth?

From your speech you can spread the goodness of truth or you can spread the badness of personal unfounded opinion(s). As in all things life, it is your choice. Who do you want to be, the person who speaks the truth or simply the person who wants others to believe what you believe simply because you believe it?

    Your life, your choice.

Pure Joy and Happiness
22/Sep/2020 08:12 AM

How often do you feel pure joy and happiness? In fact, do you ever feel pure joy and happiness?

Most people, the only time they feel a sense of joy and happiness is when they are getting exactly what they want in any specific moment of time. This gift of joy is given very externally. They want something, they get, and so they feel happy.

The problem with this style of emotional stimuli is, however, that then all things are dominated by external circumstances. You want, you get, you are happy. You want, you don't get, you are not.

If you think about this, and this style of Joy Stimulation, isn't that how you have passed through your entire life? You lived, you existed, but they only time you were truly happy is when you got what you wanted. But, is this the only way life can be lived? Is this the only way you can feel happiness?

Here's the experiment for the day: Right now, be happy. Take a moment, close your eyes, go inside your mind, and find that place where joy and happiness exists.

This place/space may take a few minutes to find because most people never seek it out. It only magically appears when, as described, you are getting something that you want. But, it is already inside of you. Find it!

The moment you go to that space of joy and happiness, that is already inside of you, you immediately realize that, yes, you can feel joy without getting that Something. You can touch that joyous experience without the need for external stimulation.

Believe me when I tell you, once you find out that you can be happy and joyous without the need for that external Something your entire life is going to turn around. No longer will you be controlled by that plaguing need to get Something to feel fulfilled.

Find that joy, find that happiness inside of you and you can touch it any time you feel the need.

Like everything else good in life it takes practice. Care enough to practice finding your internal joy and your entire life can become so much better.

Helping with No Agenda
21/Sep/2020 04:58 PM

I often speak and write about how people should help one another. Sometimes people contact me and tell about the help they are providing. Sometimes via TV, radio, the internet, social media, or other sources I hear about someone talking about the help they have given someone or something. But, the more I hear about it, the more it becomes self-evident that people are not helping simply to help, they are helping to gain something out of their helping.

It is a very simple thing to think about. Go back in your mind and think about a time when you helped someone. Why did you do it? In virtually all cases, (if you are honest with yourself), the reason you helped someone is that you either wanted to gain something from that person from your helping them or you wanted to be praised as being a good person by your helping. How many times in your life have you helped anyone simply to help them with no ego or no hope for any desired outcome as part of the mix?

People commonly falsely believe they are helping when they are simply attempting to get their own or someone else's agenda enacted. But, that is not really helping. Sure, it may be aiding your cause or your political party—it may even be helping a person win a battle over another person. But, that kind of helping is all Ego and Self Based. It does not arise from a pure sense of giving. It comes hand-in-hand with an agenda.

True helping, truly helping, is a process where you remove yourself from the equation. It is a space where you are doing simply to make the all and the everything of someone or everyone a little bit better. The main component in True Helping is that you have nothing to gain. You want or expect nothing from the person or persons you are helping and you do not desire to receive pride or praise because of your helping.

The person who truly helps tells no one that they are helping. They do not announce it and/or broadcast their helping to the world or to any individual. They simply do the deed. They simply help. They expect no reward and they turn one down if it is offered.

True helping is silent.

When You Make a Milkshake
21/Sep/2020 09:54 AM

There are so many people doing so many things in this world. For each of them, what they are doing is All Important. What they are feeling is the only thing they are feeling. But, is what they are doing, what they are feeling, what they care about important to anyone else?

I was having breakfast yesterday; sitting in this outdoor courtyard. At least here in L.A., outdoors is the only place you can eat in restaurants right now due to the COVID-19 coronavirus pandemic. No indoor dining. But, that was fine, the weather was nice, the outdoor patio space of this restaurant was nice, and all was going along as it should.

While I was sitting there, I got a text from a friend of mine. Jokingly he said, *"You're birthday's coming up, where do you want to go?"* I smiled. I mean, my favorite cities in the world are Tokyo, Hong Kong, and Jerusalem. Any of those locations would have been fine. But, as I don't hang with the Private Jet Set Crew and as COVID-19 cases are again rising all across the globe, equaling travel-restrictions, lock-downs, self-quarantines, and the like, so there is little chance I could go to any of those places. But, the question did make me smile.

I realized I was sitting there in the courtyard of the restaurant, surround by people. Each of them sat there eating and talking about their own melodrama. Each of them was living their own life, defined, at least in part, by what we are all defined by right now, COVID-19. Add to that all that other stuff that inhabits all of our lives.

I realized, I could have been anywhere. …Anywhere in the world. No matter where I found myself, people are all the same. They are all thinking about what they are thinking about. They are all focused on themselves and the people and the things they care about and the people and the things that are affecting them. But, for most, they are only focused on themselves. So, it was nice to realize that someone cared enough about me to hit me up with a text about where I wished I could be on my birthday, even if there was no way I could go there.

* * *

21/Sep/2020 06:34 AM

What makes you feel good?

Does what makes you feel good involve somebody else or other people?

What affect does your feeling good have on those other people?

What makes you feel bad?

Does what makes you feel bad involve somebody else or other people?

What affect does your feeling bad have on those other people?

* * *
19/Sep/2020 12:04 PM

If you feel that you must continually broadcast to the world that you are something special doesn't that mean that you are the only one who believes it?

* * *
18/Sep/2020 11:44 AM

When you misunderstand what somebody says is it their fault for not explaining themselves correctly or your fault for not understanding what they are trying to say?

Defending What is Yours
AKA Everybody's Everything
18/Sep/2020 08:59 AM

There has somehow become this belief that people should not be allowed to defend what is theirs. We have seen this in all of the recent protests leading to riots that have taken place. It seems, whenever someone steps up to defend what is theirs they are condemned for their action. But, if something belongs to someone shouldn't they have the right to defend and protect it? Moreover, what has happened to the mind of modern society that they now believe they can simply take what they want even when they did nothing to earn it?

For anyone who has ever had anything stolen from them, they understand the emotional pain of this occurrence. For anyone who has ever had any unwanted violence unleashed on them, they know the pain of being attacked. Most people, even if they have not personally experienced one of these unwanted incidents, understands that taking what is not theirs is wrong, destroy someone else's something is not right, hurting anyone should not be done. Yet, it seems, that there has been an entire culture born where stealing, hurting, and destruction is recognized as some sort of achievement.

Throughout history, those who have stolen have been condemned and punished. Now, though that style of consequence is still active, there is an entire cultural where it is respected. When someone is caught or taken to task for their stealing, damaging, destroying, or hurting, an entire throng of people come to their defense. Is that right?

At the essence of every person, at the crux of every culture is a sense of morality. An understanding of what is right and what is wrong. Certainly, this understanding evolves through time, but what is good, right, and honorable should not. Taking what is not yours should not be seen as right. Destroying what is not yours should not be condoned. Hurting, someone/anyone, on any level, should be condemned. Why is it not?

The problem has evolved in that mob mentality has been accentuated by social media. It is kind of like when the football team you like wins against the opponents you do not, there is a sense of excitement. But, why do you like that one football team? Why do you dislike the other? Do you ever contemplate this? Do you ever study your emotions and why you feel them? Do you ever ask yourself why do you allow you emotions to cause you to say what you say and to do what you do? If you don't, you are living a life not defined by an enhanced sense of goodness, self-knowledge, and virtue. If this is the case, this is where a life defined by hurt and damage to others is unleashed.

Do you believe that someone else, someone that you do not know—that you never met, has the right to take what is yours? Do you believe that someone else has the right to damage your property? Do you believe that someone else has the right to hurt you? Most probably you do not believe that someone has the right to do any of those things to you. So, why do you or those people you know or support; why do they have the right to do it?

If you treat people the way you want to be treated all life becomes so much better. Don't steal, don't take what isn't yours, don't destroy, don't hurt and think how much better everything becomes.

The world begins with you. The world begins with what you choose to do. Develop the mind and the mindset to do good.

***

18/Sep/2020 07:00 AM

How do you measure your day?

Autobiography of a Lie
17/Sep/2020 06:56 AM

Who are you? Are you the person who you tell the world you are or are you the inner being inside your human form that thinks, that feels, the exists, that translated reality via your own definition? And, do you know who you truly are?

Most people are lost in the projection of who they want themselves to be seen as by the external world. They want to be viewed as a something—they want whom they are (Their Projected Self) to be seen as that thing. From this, a world of deception is given birth to.

Think about the people you have known. Think about the people you have read or have heard about. Who are they and why do you think they are what they are? In almost all cases the reason you believe you know who they are is because someone has told you. Either they personally told you what they think, how they feel, what they like, what they don't like or someone else has talked about them; explaining to you who and what they are. But, in all of these cases, how do you know if what they are saying is true?

Think about the last time you told a lie. Why did you tell it? Moreover, did you even question yourself on the deep realms of your self-consciousness why you were about to lie or did the lie simply come from your lips with no internal conversation about how what you were doing was wrong?

Most people who lie never possess the inner level of refined consciousness to question their action. They just do it. They just lie. Why do they lie? The answer to that question could be explained via various methods of logic and an untold number of reasonings but it will almost never be truly understood by the person who is telling you the lie. Why? Because they do not possess the inner honesty to truly delve deeply into their self, know their self, analyze their self, and be able to present an honest conclusion.

Think about the people you have known who have lied to you. These lies may have been small or they may have been very large; but you were told something about someone, you believed it, and then it turned out to be a fabrication. Then what? How did that lie change your understanding of that individual and how did it cause you to react to them? …How did you react to them before you knew they lied and how did you react to them after?

Most people when they are caught in a lie, lie to cover up the fact that they have lied. Some people are pathologic liars. They lie about anything/everything and they do it while looking you directly in your eyes. They are so lost into being a liar that they cannot or do not care about the negative impact their lies may have on the life of other people. It is their drug. A lair is who they are.

All this being said, think about the people you know, think about the people you have heard about, think about the people you think about, ponder how much you know about them is based in a reality that you have lived with them (The Truth) and how much of it is based simply upon what they told you about themselves or what you have heard about them from someone else. Think about if all you believe about is a person is a lie, then what? Think about if one small thing you believe about a person is a lie, then what? Think about the lies you have told other people about yourself (large or small), now what?

You initially know a person by the autobiography they present to you. Yes, over time you develop experiences that you have lived with them, but what are those experiences initially based upon? They are based upon what you believe a person to be. What if what you believe them to be is not who they truly are at all? What if they have lied? Then what?

* * *
16/Sep/2020 01:59 PM

You can know who a person truly is by the lies they tell.

* * *
16/Sep/2020 08:37 AM

If nobody sees you does it matter what you look like?

THE ZEN

www.ingramcontent.com/pod-product-compliance
Lightning Source LLC
Chambersburg PA
CBHW060115170426
43198CB00010B/904